Ethnicity and Social Work Practice

Ethnicity and Social Work Practice

CAROLE B. COX

PAUL H. EPHROSS

New York Oxford
OXFORD UNIVERSITY PRESS
1998

Oxford University Press

Oxford New York
Athens Aukland Bangkok Bogotá Bombay Buenos Aires
Calcutta Cape Town Dar es Salaam Delhi Florence Hong Kong
Istanbul Karachi Kuala Lumpur Madras Madrid Melbourne
Mexico City Nairobi Paris Singapore Taipei Tokyo Toronto

and associated companies in
Berlin Ibadan

Published by Oxford University Press, Inc.,
198 Madison Avenue, New York, New York 10016

Library of Congress Cataloging-in-Publication Data
Cox, Carole B. Ethnicity and social work practice / Carole Cox & Paul H. Ephross.
p. cm. Includes bibliographical references and index.
ISBN 0-19-509930-3 (cloth). — ISBN 0-19-509931-1 (pbk.)
1. Social work with minorities—United States. 2. Ethnic groups —
United States. 3. Ethnicity—United States. I. Ephross, Paul H.
II. Title.
HV3176.C69 1997 362.84′00973—dc20 96-34098
CIP

9 8 7 6 5 4 3 2 1

Printed in the United States of America
on acid-free paper

To our grandparents and parents who taught us to treasure our ethnic heritage, to Colin and Joan with whom we share it, and to Amanda, Susannah, Sara, Peter, and David who continue it.

Contents

Preface

The issue of ethnicity in American society has become a major concern as immigration, the rights of immigrants, and demands for equality by minorities have called for increasing attention. This attention is not confined to the political arena, where lawmakers are struggling to devise what they believe is appropriate legislation. Increasingly, social workers find themselves working with clients from diverse backgrounds and cultures. Their ability to work effectively with these populations is dependent upon a myriad of factors reflective of ethnicity, and it is these factors that this book addresses.

Knowledge and understanding of ethnicity and the ways in which it can influence individuals' perceptions, and their responses to problems and to help and helpers are critical for effective practice, whether with individuals, groups, families, or communities. But knowledge alone is not sufficient for establishing social work relationships with these clients. To a large extent, the development of these relationships depends upon the sensitivity of the practitioner to the culture and traditions of the client and the ways in which these may influence behaviors.

Rather than attempting to address these issues by describing the traits of specific ethnic groups, we present the model of an ethnic lens. It is through this lens that ethnic group members are likely to perceive society, problems, the helping process, and the social workers who would assist them. At the same time, social work practitioners perceive the ethnic group through their own lenses ground in and shaped by their own experiences and beliefs. As we discuss throughout the book, the effectiveness of practice and the establishment of a valid social work relationship will depend to a large extent on the clarity of these lenses.

Using this model as a framework, we examine the major areas of practice in which social workers are involved—work with individuals, families, groups, and communities—and the contexts in which they work—social service agencies, health care, and social policy. We feel that this approach reduces the potential for stereotyping that can result from efforts to describe particular ethnic groups and their characteristics. Although such descriptions are useful for basic learning about cultural experiences and traits, they may also impair relationships as the worker's expectations cloud the ethnic lens. In these situations, the uniqueness of the individual client is difficult to see.

Ethnicity is a complex phenomenon involving many components and varying degrees of allegiance. At the same time, as American society becomes more and more diverse, there is a pressing need for social workers who are ethnically sensitive and skilled. Our intention is to underscore the breadth of ethnicity and its manifestations so that social workers are comfortable and effective in working with many diverse populations.

Carole B. Cox
Paul H. Ephross
June 1996

Ethnicity and Social Work Practice

1

Setting the Stage: Ethnicity in American Society

In recent years, as American society has struggled with the nature of its own identity and boundaries, ethnicity and ethnic group membership have become major concerns. Public policy, programs, services, and the media have become noticeably aware of and sensitive to the issues of ethnic and cultural diversity. Nowhere has this sensitivity been more pronounced than within the social work profession whose foremost mission is meeting the welfare needs of society. Social policies and services have become increasingly responsible for addressing the needs of those whose very diversity can be a major factor in their social vulnerability.

However, such concerns are not a new phenomenon in social work. In fact, the roots of social work practice in this country, formed in the Charity Organization Society (COS) and Settlement House movement and in the attempts of immigrant and minority groups to create their own services, were closely tied to meeting the needs of those seeking to adapt to and find their places in American society.

Social Work and Ethnicity

The first COS was organized in 1877 in Buffalo, New York, as a means to dealing rationally with needy individuals and families. Rather than simply distributing aid, the organization maintained records of applicants and agencies. However, the COS closely reflected the philosophy of the age, believing that poverty was due to moral depravity and defects. The abundance of America meant that poverty could only be attributed to sinfulness, immorality, and laziness. In addition, excessive relief giving was to be guarded against as it would only further undermine the motivation to work. Thus, the societies also acted as means of social control as they guarded the conservative middle class and civilization against the unrest perpetrated by poverty (Lubove, 1971).

Through the society's own "friendly visitors," each applicant for assistance was investigated and the worthy poor were distinguished from the unworthy. The motto, "Not Alms but a Friend" underscored the work of these visitors as they gave advice and acted as examples to the poor as a means of helping them to become self-sufficient. But the work of these visitors could not ignore the special challenges associated with the plight of the immigrants.

From the 1880s on American cities became the focus of large concentrations of immigrants eager to settle in the new country. These immigrants concentrated in major cities such as New York, Philadelphia, Boston, and Chicago, dramatically increasing both the numbers and the diversity of their populations. Between 1866 and 1917, more than 200,000 Europeans entered the United States each year, with most settling in these cities. In 1910, in the eight largest cities of America, more than a third of the population was foreign born (Trattner, 1974).

For the most part these persons were unskilled, poor, and unable to speak English. The most visible of these immigrants were those who concentrated in the centers of these cities, lived in the poorest housing, and lacked the basic amenities common to the majority of the American population. These persons placed severe challenges on the friendly visitors because their languages and customs presented barriers to involvement. This challenge was clearly described in 1892 by the Associated Charities of Boston: "But the Italians are truly foreigners to us. We do not speak a common language, our standards have no meaning to them, and we may well doubt whether they have any applicability" (p. 11).

The most influential figure of the charity organization society movement, Mary Richmond, in her classic text *Social Diagnosis*, published in 1917, emphasized the importance of understanding diversity in social work practice. In working with foreign-born clients, social workers could attribute specific traits or characteristics to their national heritage, ignore these characteristics, or apply the same "standards of measures" to them that were applied to all Americans. Helping these immigrants to become American meant helping them to overcome traits that were incompatible with their new society.

In contrast to the COS, which focused on individual traits as key factors in poverty while indeed working with ethnic groups, the settlement house movement of the late 1880s focused on the role of social and economic conditions as the major contributors to need. The settlement movement was concerned with the issue of social, rather than individual, reform as it worked to improve the conditions contributing to poverty. Settlement workers lived in the slums and ghettos, where they could work alongside those they sought to help and thus help socialize them to American values and society.

Settlement houses legitimated ethnicity in several ways. Because the movement saw neighborhoods as basic social units for teaching the skills necessary for social action and citizenship, and the vast majority of urban neighborhoods were organized and defined by ethnicity, ethnic identification could not be ignored. Sometimes grudgingly, sometimes more enthusiastically, settlements helped neighborhoods to celebrate ethnic "national days," worked as forces for interethnic tolerance, and promoted the concept that becoming American did not mean the renouncing of a cultural heritage and traditions.

While recognizing diversity, the settlement movement sought to make the immigrants into Americans, although the attitudes and perceptions of the settlement leaders varied widely. Whereas Jane Addams espoused cultural pluralism, recognized distinct needs of immigrants, and valued their cultures, Robert Woods of Boston's South End House saw immigrants as barriers to national unity and was an advocate for immigration restrictions (Iglehart and Becerra, 1995).

It is also important to remember that immigrants and African Americans were not completely dependent upon the assistance of either the COS or the Settlement Movement as they developed their own self-help organizations. Often based in churches and related to the church's essential mission, these programs often antedate the COS and the Settlement Houses. Programs of the African Methodist Episcopal Church (founded in Philadelphia in the 1790s), ethnically defined youth organizations of Roman Catholic parishes founded throughout the 19th century, the Young Men's (and later Young Women's) Hebrew Associations dating from 1859, and the African-American settlement houses in Chicago and many other cities exemplify this trend.

The Waves of Immigration

America is a nation of immigrants, but absorbing and integrating these immigrants has not been easy. For the most part, the country's pluralistic character has shown a remarkable ability to accept diversity. Indeed, this acceptance and the resulting heterogeneity of the people are among the country's most prominent features. But, at the same time, whether the country is a "melting pot" that aims to unite all groups through common values and goals or a mosaic in which the groups' unique cultures and traditions are exhorted remains an issue of concern and frequently one of contention.

African Americans, the first large group of immigrants, were brought here involuntarily. The first Africans arrived in Virginia in the early days of the colony, probably as indentured servants, a position shared with many of the whites in the colony (Takaki, 1993). However, in 1661 the Virginia Assembly institutionalized slavery, eventually defining a slave as property. With this definition, and driven by concerns over discontent among white laborers, landowners and planters were instrumental in the development of a racially subordinated labor force (Takaki, 1993). As new laws dictated the interactions between whites and blacks, subordinating blacks to a lower status, the framework for subsequent ethnic relationships was established.

The Africans were followed by northern, and then central and eastern, Europeans, who in contrast to the first immigrants, came voluntarily to America seeking refuge from economic and religious persecution. By the time of the first federal census in 1790, 3,172,444 whites and 757,208 blacks resided in the 13 original states and in Vermont, Kentucky, and Tennessee. Almost half of the white population, 49%, was English, with the next largest group being German, followed by the Scots (Archdeacon, 1983). The saliency of ethnicity during that period is reflected by the identification of the Irish as three distinct ethnic groups, Scotch Irish, English Irish, and Celtic Irish.

In the next hundred years, as the nation expanded westward and cities were built, new groups of immigrants came to America because revolutions, wars, famines, and the promise of economic opportunity impelled many to leave their native homelands. Between 1820, when immigration numbers were first recorded, and 1890, the centennial of the first census, nearly 15 million immigrants arrived in the United States (Archdeacon, 1983).

As essential as these immigrants were for the development and expansion of the new country, their acceptance was not easy, particularly for those perceived as most different or foreign. In the case of African Americans, there is ample evidence that the strategy of whites, intellectually and politically, was to deny their humanity, to say nothing of their equality. Thus, at different times, political compromises were arrived at that counted a slave as a fraction of a person for the purposes of determining population and representation in Congress.

Initially, concerns regarding the potential threats that these persons might pose to the political stability of the country acted as barriers to integration. The influx of immigrants in the 19th century caused further concern: that the social order itself and the established way of life was endangered. In fact, this way of life *was* being threatened, but the main culprit was industrialization and not the immigrants supplying the labor.

Unfortunately, the ills of society could easily be blamed on these disadvantaged newcomers, who concentrated in the slums of urban centers. With little opportunity to rise out of poverty, immigrants were generally forced to live in tenements and overcrowded housing. Poor living conditions, lack of sanitation, different languages, and strange behaviors and customs fueled American contempt for immigrants groups, who were perceived as both different and threatening to society. These threats were heightened by fears that immigrants were taking jobs away from native-born Americans.

The cynical and provocative use of immigrants, whether from abroad or from the poverty-stricken rural South, as strikebreakers to destroy the nascent union-organizing movement in the late 19th and early 20th centuries was met with violence fueled equally by racism and bigotry on the one hand and by deliberately provoked anger on the other. Some of the most shameful race riots in America's history had their immediate causes in this kind of political manipulation by industry of poverty-stricken, undereducated, and unsophisticated members of an oppressed minority (Quarles,1982).

So strong were these fears and anxieties of nativists in the 19th century that they were reflected in the policies of political parties. The Know-Nothings, a political movement in the 1850s, sought the elimination of all foreigners and Roman Catholics from public office, the establishment of a 21-year naturalization period for all aliens, the deportation of foreign paupers and criminals, Bible reading in the public schools, and the preservation of Protestant domination in all areas of public life (Spann, 1981).

Immigration from Africa and northern and western Europe peaked before the 20th century, to be surpassed in the late 19th and early 20th centuries by immigration from southern and eastern Europe. During the last half of the 20th century immigrants have increasingly been from the Americas and Asia. Asian immigration—Chinese, Koreans, Vietnamese, Filipinos, and Indians—increased substantially after 1970 and, since 1981, has exceeded that from any other part of the world (Hraba, 1994).

Slightly more than 1.1 million immigrants enter the United States each year, with undocumented immigration contributing about 200,000 to 300,000 additional persons annually (Fix and Passel, 1994). About a third of the undocumented immigrants are from Mexico, with slightly fewer from Central America and the Carribean (Warren, 1993). The majority of both legal and illegal immigrants live in six states: California, New York, Texas, Florida, New Jersey, and Illinois.

Without the expansion of industrial growth, which managed to absorb earlier waves of immigrants, nativist and anti-immigrant sentiments have risen. Concern over the nation's ability to absorb these immigrants and the demands they may place on health and social welfare services and benefits such as Aid for Dependent Children (AFDC) and Supplemental Security Income (SSI) have become major political issues.

Ethnic Identity

Ethnic groups generally share a common culture, a sense of identity as a subgroup or community with a consciousness of kind or a "we" feeling, ascribed membership by birth or descent, a sense of historical continuity and a common past, and a feeling of attachment to a common ancestral territory (Marger, 1994). In addition, they display a sense of ethnocentrism, in that members regard their way as the correct way of behavior. In this way ethnicity, as it fosters solidarity, can also foster suspicion and dissension (Khinduka, 1995).

The complexity of ethnicity is underscored through its multiple and varying definitions and interpretations. Max Weber (1961) defines ethnic groups as persons with a sense of belief in their common descent, because of either physical type or customs or both, or because of memories of colonization and emigration. Gordon (1964) defines an ethnic group as individuals with a shared sense of peoplehood based on race, religion, or national origin. Shibutani and Kwan (1965) expand this definition by including the perception of the individual and others: "an ethnic group consists of those who conceive of themselves as being alike by virtue of their common ancestry, real or fictitious, or are so regarded by others" (p. 47).

Barth (1969) emphasizes the need for distinction between the ethnic organization of a group and the ethnic identification of individuals and the culture by which an ethnic group may be defined. However, such identification may in itself not be genuine. Thus, Gans (1979) distinguishes "symbolic ethnicity" as an attempt to feel ethnic but with no real commitment by the individual to ethnicity, which reflects specific actions and experiences.

However, ethnicity may be a moot concern without other groups that differ from the particular group and with which the specific ethnic group interacts. Cohen (1974) includes the role of interaction in his definition, "a collectivity of people who a) share some patterns of normative behavior and b) form a part of a larger population interacting with people from other collectivities within the framework of a social system" (p. ix). Without a social system that contains different populations, the concept of ethnicity is meaningless.

Finally, it is this larger social system that provides much of the meaning of ethnicity. "Ethnic identity requires the maintenance of sufficiently consistent behavior to enable others to place an individual or group in some given social category, thus permitting appropriate interactive behavior" (De Vos, 1975, p. 374). It is in these interactions with the greater social system that social work's role has become most apparent. Many factors can affect the interactions of ethnic groups with the larger social systems of which they are a part and to which they relate. However, in ethnically heterogeneous societies, ethnicity is often a basis for political power and social stratification.

Ethnicity has both objective and subjective attributes (Khinduka, 1995). Common language, religion, and traditions are shared objective attributes, while a sense of identity, belonging, and solidarity are its subjective reflections (Van den Berghe, 1981). At the same time, ethnic solidarity is frequently politicized, as it forms the basis for group competition and pursuits of power.

Although the nation celebrates cultural pluralism through ethnic festivals and holidays, there is also concern about the extent to which these ethnic groups are able to assimilate into and accommodate with American culture and society without having to give up their unique differences. Meeting the diverse needs of these populations necessitates sensitive policies and services appropriate to particular cultural needs and interests. Without this sensitivity such policies, and the programs and services based upon them, are likely either to play insignificant roles in the lives of these persons or, in some instances, actually to foster alienation.

Defining Ethnicity

The term *ethnicity* connotes both psychological and social identity. From a psychological framework, ethnicity refers to the way in which the individual develops a sense of self. Within an Eriksonian perspective, a child develops a sense of identity and personality through the resolution of developmental crisis and life stages (Erikson, 1963). The ways in which these crises are resolved are in large part dependent upon the models of behavior existent in a particular society and setting. Cultural values and expectations shape social identity through their influences on the decisions the child makes. As an example, the resolution of autonomy will differ between cultures where adolescents are expected to work and those where they are not permitted to work. Consequently, the need for autonomy will be identical but the manner in which it is enacted will differ.

Individuals who belong to an ethnic group are governed by the values and normative expectations adhered to by the group members. Such forces shape ethnic identity. But this identity is not rigid. The factors shaping identity vary in salience to the individual. Thus, first-generation immigrants generally adhere more closely to these values and norms than do third-generation, who have adapted to those of the greater society. The degree to which a person continues to act within the norms of a specific group will in a large part determine the role ethnicity plays in his or her identity.

Ethnic groups are bound by shared culture, the symbols and traditions which guide individual member's expectations and actions. Culture within society systematizes interactions, as individuals learn what to expect from each other and how they themselves should behave and interact. Culture is not only shared but also is inherited and passed down, so that all members of an ethnic group learn to behave and interact in prescribed manners. A group's culture is reflected in symbols such as language, food, dress, art, music, values, and ways of interacting. Ethnic symbols therefore reflect the uniqueness of a group while also being critical determinants of individuals' thinking and behaviors. If wealth is perceived as a measure of worth or status, group members will strive to achieve it, whereas if it is perceived as a symbol of decadence or self-aggrandizement, it is likely to be shunned.

As culture is reflected through values and patterns of interaction it is also enacted through the roles individuals play. Cultural expectations are conveyed through norms that govern behaviors and are often most apparent in the ways social roles are enacted. Thus, men may be expected to be the main providers in the family, to make the decisions, and to discipline the children, while women may be expected to adhere to these decisions and to focus on the home. The elderly may be revered as conveyors of wisdom and tradition or shunned as useless, while children may be indulged or ignored.

Equally important as the roles people play are the ways in which they are expected to express emotions and sentiments. Culture may dictate that emotions are kept hidden and that the individual should not display any sentiments that could be interpreted as offensive to others. Thus, anger or disappointment are kept hidden. On the other hand, other cultures expect that emotions, including anger and love, are freely exhibited. Moreover, the manner in which such sentiments are displayed can also be dictated by cultural expectations.

In order to understand the distinctiveness of cultures, it is important to begin with an identification of those factors associated with ethnicity and hence with group values and behaviors. Steward (1972) identifies five components of culture that need to be considered in understanding cultural assumptions and values:

1. *Activity*. How do people approach activity? How important are goals in life? Who makes decisions? What is the nature of problem solving?
2. *Definition of social relations*. How are roles defined? How do people relate to those whose status is different? How are sex roles defined? What is the meaning of friendship?
3. *Motivation*. What is the achievement orientation of the culture? Is co-operation or competition emphasized?
4. *Perception of the world*. What is the predominant world view? What is the predominant view on human nature? What is the predominant view on the nature of truth? How is time defined? What is the nature of property?
5. *Perception of self and the individual*. How is self defined? Where is a person's identity determined? What is the nature of the individual? What kinds of persons are valued and respected?

Kluckhohn and Strodtbeck (1961) offer five further categories of components which should be explored in efforts to understand cultural values and attitudes:

1. *Time*. Is the orientation based on the past, the present, or the future?
2. *Human relations*. Are individuals, collateral relationships, or lineal relationships valued most?
3. *Human activity*. Is the focus on doing, being, or becoming?
4. *Human nature*. At birth, are people considered basically good, bad, neutral, or mixed?
5. *Supernatural*. Is the relationship with the supernatural one of control, subordination, or harmony?

There are various ways of measuring ethnicity. One way utilizes a none–some scale, viewing ethnicity as a nominal characteristic—one either is Italian American or is not. Another measure views ethnicity and ethnic identification as ordinal characteristics—some persons whom others consider Italian Americans or Puerto Ricans may not consider themselves as ethnic or may do so only on specific occasions. They may also perceive ethnicity as affecting them only in limited areas of their lives such as during holidays. Others, such as Orthodox Jews, consider ethnicity a major aspect of their identity, a central organizing factor around which all other experiences and behaviors are shaped. In this sense, ethnicity may be experienced as the most important distinct characteristic of their psychological and social lives.

Two approaches are used to measure the intensity or saliency of ethnicity to the individual. These are broadly characterized as objective and subjective. Indeed, there have even been efforts to assign numerical values to the salience of ethnicity for people, groups, and communities. If the numbers are viewed as being in a quantitative relationship to each other, they act as an interval scale. The varying types of measurements indicate the importance, and at the same time the difficulty, posed by trying to measure the intensity of ethnicity.

Objective measures seek to assess behaviors which are viewed as indicators of ethnicity and ethnic identification. Such indicators are shown below.

Behavior	Indicator
Ethnic foods	Frequency, occasions, preparations, cere monies.
Language	Spoken at home; taught to children; used in worship, used by the media.
Religious institutions	Congregations with same ethnic background, role of institution in life, ethnicity of clergy.
Marriage	Within ethnic group, sanctions against deviance.
Family forms	Relationships, roles, kinship.
Community	Defined boundaries, interactions, supports, clustering.
Education	Schools, patterns, extra (ethnic) after-school classes.
Social roles	Influenced by traditional norms and expectations.
Help-seeking behavior	From whom, under what circumstances.

Although not exhaustive, the behaviors and indicators in the above list suggest the many areas of life that may be affected by ethnicity and ethnic identity. All of these areas impact on the social work profession and practice. The chapters of this book are intended to clarify this impact, as well as the means by which social workers can become most sensitive to the role ethnicity plays in both their own lives and those of their clients. A word about the value stance of this book seems in order.

The authors, one the granddaughter of immigrants and the other the native-born son of immigrants, view ethnicity in all its diversity as enriching the lives of individuals and their communities. Without in any way minimizing the stresses and strains that accompany acculturation or the driving and often painful desires to "fit in," without waxing maudlin over the contributions people of various ethnic backgrounds have made to all aspects of American life, and in full awareness of the sorrow that can accompany the translating of traditional ethnic and national hatreds to the United States, this book is ethnic-affirmative. The relevance of this stance for social work will become clear in the following chapters which discuss in depth specific fields and modes of practice.

Our sense of uniqueness, of being rooted in one space to one group, comes from our membership in families. When we examine ourselves, we find that who we are and who we can become depend in great part upon who we started out to be. This is found within our families. Ethnicity cannot be separated from families (McAdoo, 1993). Almost all families may be considered to be from one or another ethnic group.

Society plays a major part in the shaping and determination of ethnicity. For, although individuals may seek to shed their ethnic identity and assimilate into the mainstream, society itself may act as a barrier. Because individuals are perceived as being different, they may be excluded from assimilation or deterred from it. They are thus encouraged or even forced to maintain an ethnic identity they no longer feel is appropriate. This situation is most frequent when ethnic groups are physically distinct from the majority population. Although they may no longer adhere to traditional cultural values, their appearance implies their difference and separation from the majority. Consequently, they are often treated according to this difference.

Differences are the basis for stereotyping and for prejudices. As persons are perceived as ethnic group members, specific behaviors are prescribed and anticipated, and stereotypes ensue. Such stereotypes engender prejudice because persons are prejudged and labeled on the basis of their characteristics. Ethnicity can easily blend into prejudice and this prejudice itself can strengthen a sense of ethnicity. As individuals are excluded from other social groups, they may be forced to maintain a strong allegiance to the ethnic culture. When Jews were excluded from clubs and neighborhoods, they tended to form their own alternative ones, which further served to keep them out of the greater society.

Moreover, persons sharing common characteristics are labeled, so they may feel compelled to behave in expected ways. Even though they may not share the values attributed to others with the same characteristics, to the extent that they are labeled "ethnic," groups may feel that they are required to partake in certain festivals or show allegiance to identified community leaders.

Ethnicity is not a constant. Its meaning and saliency alter with generations. First-generation immigrants tend to adhere strongly to ethnic values and traditions, but these often become weakened with subsequent generations. In many instances, such trends can lead to family tensions and conflicts, as children shun traditional behaviors for those of the new society. In these instances, the new roles do not include, and may even scorn, the old behaviors.

Ethnicity also varies with the life course, as there are specific age-related norms for behaviors. Thus, child rearing may be strongly influenced by traditional values that stress modes of discipline and types of education that shape the behaviors of young children. As children age, have more interactions with others outside of their ethnic group, they often find the new, desired roles are incompatible with the traditional expectations.

In the middle years, people frequently try to accommodate ethnic norms and expectations with their "nonethnic" selves. How salient ethnicity is to the identity of the individual will depend on many factors such as personal ties and sense of commitment, community, and even social class. In the later years, many find a renewed interest in "ethnicity," which can become a major source of support as they become more dependent. Consequently, many seek retirement communities or nursing homes that serve primarily one ethnic population.

Race

Ethnicity is not the same as race, although the two terms are often used interchangeably. Members of ethnic groups sharing common traditions, heritage, and even language are often indistinct from the majority of society. Frequently, their ethnicity is apparent only during specific occasions or when they choose to display it. Thus, parades and festivals—Italian-American, Irish-American, or Lithuanian—are occasions when individuals pronounce their ethnic identity.

Members of specific races are generally consistently confronted with their identity and are not permitted the freedom of determining when to display it. Their physical characteristics, often in conjunction with their language and traditions connote their ethnic ties. Prejudgments are made on the basis of the perceptions of others in society, and these prejudgements are major determinants of these individuals' roles and behaviors. Histories of discrimination and exclusion from society can strengthen attitudes and behaviors of these individuals as the boundaries into the greater society remain impermeable. Accordingly, membership in a specific race can strengthen a sense of ethnic identity.

A plethora of ethnic groups can be subsumed within one racial group and thus, to assume homogeneity can ignore important distinctions. Thus, the three largest groups, blacks, whites, and Asians, include within them many ethnic groups with their own experiences, traditions, values, norms, and even languages. But, to the extent that these people are perceived as being homogeneous by the greater society, these separate identities are often overlooked.

The regard attributed to a group is closely related to the values of the majority in society. To the extent that the group is perceived as adhering to these values, their acceptance is easier. Asians, with their focus on education, strong regard for family, and industriousness, have been perceived as the "model" minority. On the other hand, the high rates of unemployment, poverty, and broken families among African Americans have been used as symbols of the group's deviance with regard to established values and behaviors.

Ethnicity and Social Class

In any discussion of ethnicity it is essential to differentiate between ethnicity and social class. Many behaviors attributed to ethnic values and norms may be responses to the social classes persons occupy. Individuals' behaviors reflect those of their niches and the resources they have available. As ethnic persons acculturate into society, these niches change, and their attitudes, values, and behaviors can be expected to alter. Although they may adhere to many traditional values, they also assume the values and, consequently, the behaviors common to others in their niches and habitats.

In working with ethnic groups, it is critical to understand which behaviors result from oppression, discrimination, and poverty and which are reflections of ethnic values and norms. Reluctance to use medical care or other social services may reflect years of poor care, long waits, and insensitive service providers. Middle-class individuals from the same ethnic groups who are accustomed to responsive and appropriate services are likely to express more willingness to use them.

However, acculturation and middle-class status do not necessarily diffuse or neutralize traditional values and behaviors. Adherence to cultural beliefs and attitudes can continue to influence individuals' actions and interactions. As an example, it is not uncommon for individuals, regardless of their social status, to continue to rely on traditional healers or herbs in treating illness. Others may strongly adhere to traditional family role definitions, which continue to influence their behaviors, interactions, and use of formal services. Distinguishing ethnic values and customs from social class contingencies remains a critical but essential task for social work.

Ethnicity, Racism, and Oppression

In examining ethnicity, it is critical to understand that it is not identical to racism. Racism is prejudice and discrimination against a specific racial or ethnic group on the basis of its racial or ethnic characteristics and group membership. Racism is an ideological perspective that one race of people is inherently superior to another race. When racism is institutionalized, it forms the basis for role assignments, role rewards, socialization, and acculturation (Williams, 1988).

In the United States, racism tends to be associated with African Americans, but at various times other racial groups—Chinese, Japanese, and Hispanics—have been the targets of racism. In the Nazi era in Germany, Jews were the target of racist policies. Racism is generally assumed to be a means for the society's dominant group to maintain power and status. In fact, those in power are those that can discriminate effectively, for they are the ones who define who is inside the group and who is outside (Kitano, 1980).

Power is a key element in racism because it affects social systems, interactions, and individual self-concepts. Through social structure, the dominant or majority group maintains its power by excluding subordinates, denying them access to resources, and establishing expectations, tasks, and functions that affect both their lifestyles and those of the dominant group, and by determining how both dominant and subordinate groups perceive themselves and others (Pinderhughes, 1988). An absence of power or the recognition of low social status further affects the individual's self-perception. When people lack the resources that can enable them to interact effectively in society, their self-esteem and self-concepts are threatened. In fact, a circular reinforcing process occurs in which political, economic, and social forces create a sense of powerlessness that undermines the skills needed to cope (Pinderhughes, 1983).

Oppression is the enactment of racism through policies and behaviors. These actions serve to exclude the targeted group from institutions, resources, and social interactions common to other groups. Oppression serves to maintain the power of whichever group is dominant and in control. History is replete with examples of oppressors becoming the oppressed and carrying out the same discriminatory and persecutory policies to which they themselves had been subjected. The recent "ethnic cleansing" in Bosnia and Croatia exemplifies the extreme to which such oppression can be carried.

Ethnicity within the Ecological Perspective

The ecological perspective has become an important framework for social work practice. This perspective views individuals as in continuous interaction with their environment, and social work practice is focused on these interactions and the ways in which they can be improved. The goal is to enhance individual functioning so that a "goodness of fit" is achieved (Germain and Gitterman, 1980).This goodness of fit occurs when stress is reduced and transactions between the individual and the environment are adaptive and nurturing. Stress itself is perceived as an imbalance between individuals and the environment resulting from an inability to achieve this fit and subsequently acting as a barrier to it.

Basic to interaction are the habitat and niche of the individual. The *habitat* is the place where the individual resides and includes both physical and social settings. Thus, the habitat is the territory occupied by the individual, including buildings, public and private places, and supports.

Habitats have boundaries and these boundaries are more or less fluid. To the extent that they are impermeable, those living within a specific habitat will share common perspectives, values, and behaviors. Persons within the specific habitat learn to interact within the norms of their own environments. As these habitats become more distinct and shape behaviors and interactions, members are at risk of become increasingly isolated from the larger society.

Stress can result as patterns of interaction within the habitat are ineffective or perceived as inappropriate for interactions with the environment outside of the habitat. In addition, as those seeking to interact with persons living in the habitat do not understand or adhere to the established patterns, these interactions are also vulnerable to being stressful and ineffective.

The immediate environment and status attributed to individuals according to their place in society is termed the *niche*. The niche is the smallest place occupied by an individual or social group, with the niche itself related to issues of power and oppression (Germain, 1985). Society shapes niches as it both labels and controls the resources available to those occupying specific statuses. Thus, ethnic and minority groups, as well as the elderly, homosexuals, feminists, and others who share identified statuses, share similar niches.

Ethnicity can be a potent force in the shaping of both niches and habitats. Oppressed ethnic groups will occupy devalued niches, which means that their interactions with society are likely to be stressful when they are deprived of status and resources. On the other hand, members of ethnic groups which control resources are likely to have little stress in their interactions. Individuals sharing a niche having attributes desired by others will be influential and powerful and will dictate interactions. Conversely, those occupying devalued niches will find stress associated with their interactions. Indian society vividly illustrates these differences through its caste system as Brahmins and Untouchables, more than being social classes, represent distinct niches that cannot be transcended.

Histories of discrimination and oppression have placed many ethnic minority groups into niches and habitats with rigid boundaries that can often restrict interactions with the greater society. Stereotyping and prejudices that contribute to this rigidity can simultaneously foster the maintenance of cultural patterns. Moreover, to the extent that these patterns are perceived as deviant to those of the greater society, ethnic groups may be further excluded.

The ecological perspective can be used to trace social work's role with ethnic groups. In working through the settlement houses and self-help organizations, social workers sought to improve the habitat of new immigrants to this country, a focus which continues in neighborhood and community centers today.

Altering the niches of ethnic persons is often more complicated. With the niche closely associated with identity and perception by others, efforts to alter it include educational, social, and psychological interventions. Moreover, these cannot be exclusively targeted on those occupying the niche. These strategies, to be most effective, must include those in the greater social systems whose attitudes and behaviors reinforce the ethnic identity of the group members.

Depending upon the field and method of social work practice, various strategies will be evoked to alter the niche of the ethnic group. Consequently, those involved in health care will seek to alter behaviors that can negatively affect health and well-being or interfere with essential medical care, while social workers involved with children and families will utilize strategies that empower families and promote the welfare of the children.

Person in Environment

Social work practice is shaped by the framework of the person in environment. Instead of focusing only on the individual or only on the environment, social work has a dual focus on the individual interacting with his or her environment. Stress occurs when this interaction is difficult or does not achieve a goodness of fit (Germain and Gitterman, 1980).

In work with ethnic groups, the person-in-environment perspective is not necessarily applicable, in that the person may not be the fundamental object of interaction. Thus, the person-in-environment framework must be expanded to meet the more complex realities of members of ethnic groups. According to the beliefs and values of the specific culture, the family, the group, the ancestors, or even the community may be the focal point of interactions. Consequently, the framework that focuses on person in environment needs expansion to encompass these varying experiences. Understanding the way in which particular ethnic cultures perceive interactions and the emphasis they place on the individual, the family, or past generations is essential if stress is to be alleviated.

The Lens Model

This book presents a model of how ethnicity affects identity and group membership, the nature of the helping process, and consequently, social work practice. The authors view ethnic identification and membership as providing lenses through which members of ethnic groups perceive ("see" and "hear") experience, attribute meanings to experiences for both themselves and others, and decide upon appropriate actions to be taken. Lenses attribute meanings to relationships with others, to experiences, and to actions.

Like all lenses, the ones provided by ethnic identity may be transparent and distortion-free, with the group and its actions and behaviors correctly viewed. This transparency offers the framework for meaningful interactions, since both the "viewer" and the ethnic group member share a common understanding of actions and behaviors.

On the other hand, the lens may be partially or entirely opaque and not permit the viewer to see the group accurately. In these instances, the lens is clouded by preconceived beliefs, attitudes, and stereotypes that obscure the viewer's sight and subsequent understanding. If meanings for actions are not shared, the opaqueness can thwart interactions.

The lens may also be reflective. In this instance, rather than increasing visibility the lens reflects back onto the perceiver his or her own beliefs, which form the basis for interpretation of the group's actions. This reflection invalidates the meaning and experiences of the others' behaviors, as they are viewed according to a framework which is not necessarily appropriate. As an example, a group's resistance to vaccinations can be treated as evidence of child neglect when, according to the beliefs of the specific group, vaccination is perceived as threatening to the child's well-being.

Finally, lenses can distort so that actions and interactions are misunderstood. Disparate experiences, values, and attitudes contribute to distorted perceptions which misunderstand or misinterpret behaviors. As an example, a reluctance to use formal services can be perceived as evidence that the individual is managing without them, is uninformed, or is resistant to change, when in fact the reluctance is due to previous negative encounters with agencies. Such lenses can create a circular pattern in which the distortion itself further excludes and alienates the group from others. As an example, if all actions of a group are perceived as indicative of indifference or callousness, the group is likely to be ignored or chastised, which can lead to further exclusion.

It is important to recognize that all lenses, those used by the ethnic group members and those used by members of the greater society, are shaped by cultural meanings, values, attitudes, and experiences. In addition, factors such as economics, power, status, and politics are influential in the grinding of the lens. In this model, the lens acts as the boundary circumscribing the niche or habitat of the ethnic group member. To the extent that the lens is transparent, interaction with the greater society is facilitated. But to the extent that this lens is opaque, such interaction can be thwarted. This book illustrates the functions of these lenses in different aspects of social work practice.

The lens is fundamental to understanding the ways in which ethnicity affects social work practice. As an example, immigrants perceived through the lens may be viewed as either contributors to or burdens on the economy. Subsequently, policies and services will reflect the dominant perception and will have major impact on these persons' lives because they affect resources and opportunities.

In addition, the very concept of being a social worker's client or of becoming a helper can be viewed through ethnic lenses and from several angles. Following are some examples of questions to be experienced and evaluated through lenses furnished and ground by ethnic identity:

1. What is social work? Who does it and why? Can one trust social workers? Which ones can be trusted and how much? What kinds of information should be shared?
2. Who asks for help? Why do they ask? What type of help do they seek? Which requests are legitimate and which are not?
3. What is the nature of the helping process?
4. Whom does one go to for help? A professional, a friend, a relative?
5. Where does one go for help? To an agency? To a church? To people "like me"?
6. What does confidentiality mean? What will happen if people know I am going for help?
7. What are the possibilities of acceptable strategies or alternatives for change? For growth? For resolving conflicts? For improving situations?
8. What can a person be expected to do for himself or herself? What are considered acts of God to which a person has no ability to respond? Are there actions or burdens which one feels expected to bear or has a moral obligation to accept?

Ethnic groups share the same needs as others in society. In a broad sense it is social work's role to assure that social policies and services address these needs and that the environments in which persons live are nurturing with opportunities and resources essential for the development of human potential. Working toward overcoming the barriers, both individual and social, that can restrict these opportunities is the major task of the profession.

Ethnicity and Social Work Values

The values of the profession as illustrated in the National Association of Social Workers (NASW) code of ethics underscore the right of self-determination of the individual (1980). However, this emphasis on the individual is itself a reflection of the values of the dominant American society. Individualism and the rights of the individual, which are fundamental to American culture, are not necessarily inherent in other cultures, in which self-determination may be an alien concept. Thus, just as person in environment does not necessarily apply to different ethnic groups, neither does the concept of self-determination. In fact, it is when the stresses become overwhelming that people of color learn to function in an autonomous manner and "go it alone." This comes not from a goal of self-actualization but from a feeling of being alone and without help (Pinderhughes, 1983)

The guiding principles of the social work profession may therefore conflict with the values of the groups we seek to serve. Understanding and sensitivity to these diverse values are required if social workers are to be effective. Some have even called for a systematic re-analysis of the principles of universal practice to determine whether they are culturally biased (Ewalt and Mokuau, 1995). At the very least, social workers must be knowledgeable about the ethnic individual's interpretation of and adherence to the values we espouse. Here, as in other areas to be discussed in this book, the lens through which we perceive and act plays a critical role in the social work relationship.

Questions for Discussion

1. Describe the beginnings of social work's involvement with ethnic groups.
2. Discuss the factors contributing to America's treatment of immigrants.
3. Discuss the ways in which ethnic culture is reflected in society.
4. How does society determine the importance of ethnicity?
5. Why is it important to distinguish between ethnicity and social class?

References

Archdeacon, T. (1983). *Becoming American: An Ethnic History.* New York: Free Press.

Associated Charities of Boston. (1892, November). *Thirteenth Annual Report*, 11–12.

Barth, F. (1969). *Ethnic Groups and Boundaries.* Boston: Little, Brown.

Cohen, A. (1974). *Urban Ethnicity.* London: Tavistock.

De Vos, G. (1975). Ethnic pluralism: Conflict and accommodation. In G. De Vos and L. Romanucci-Ross (Eds.), *Ethnic Identity: Cultural Continuities and Change* (pp. 5–41). Palo Alto, CA: Mayfield.

Erikson, E. (1963). *Childhood and Society* (2nd ed.). New York: W. W. Norton.

Ewalt, P., and Mokuau, N. (1995). Self-determination from a Pacific perspective. *Social Work, 40*, 168–175.

Fix, M., and Passel, J. (1994). *Immigration and Immigrants: Setting the Record Straight.* Washington, DC: Urban Institute Press.

Gans, H. (1979). Symbolic ethnicity: The future of ethnic groups and cultures in America. *Ethnic and Racial Studies, 2*, 1–20.

Germain, C. (1985). The place of community work within an ecological approach to social work practice. In S. Taylor and R. Roberts (Eds.), *Theory and Practice of Community Social Work.* New York: Columbia University Press.

Germain, C., and Gitterman, A. (1980). *The Life Model of Social Work Practice.* New York: Columbia University Press.

Gordon, M. (1964). *Assimilation in American Life*. New York: Oxford University Press.

Hraba, J. (1994). *American Ethnicity*, 2nd edition. Itasca, IL: F. E. Peacock.

Iglehart, A., and Becerra, R. (1995). *Social Services and the Ethnic Community.* Boston: Allyn and Bacon.

Khinduka, S. (1995). Ethnic conflicts: Can anything be done? *Social Development Issues*, *17*, 1–18.

Kitano, H. (1980). *Race Relations.* Englewood Cliffs, NJ: Prentice Hall.

Kluckhohn, F., and Strodtbeck, F. (1961). *Variations in Value Orientations.* Evanston, IL: Row, Peterson.

Lubove, R. (1971). *The Professional Altruist.* Cambridge, MA: Harvard University Press.

Marger, M. (1994). *Race and Ethnic Relations: American and Global Perspectives* (4th ed.). Belmont, CA: Wadsworth.

McAdoo, H. (1993). *Family Ethnicity: Strength in Diversity.* Newbury Park, CA: Sage.

National Association of Social Workers. (1980). *Code of Ethics of the National Association of Social Workers.* Silver Spring, MD: Author.

Pinderhughes, E. (1988). Significance of culture and power in the human behavior curriculum, In C. Jacobs and D. Bowles (Eds.), *Ethnicity and Race: Critical Concepts in Social Work* (pp. 152–166). Silver Spring, MD: National Association of Social Workers.

Pinderhughes, E. B. (1983). Empowerment for our clients and for ourselves. *Social Casework*, *64*, 331–338.

Quarles, B. (1982). A. Philip Randolph: Labor leader at large. In John H. Franklin and August Meier (Eds.), *Black Leaders of the Twentieth Century* (pp. 139–166). Urbana, IL: University of Illinois Press.

Reimers, D. (1985). *Still the Golden Door.* New York: Columbia University Press.

Richmond, M. (1917). *Social Diagnosis.* New York: Russell Sage Foundation.

Shibutani, T., and Kwan, K. (1965). *Ethnic Stratification.* New York: Macmillan.

Sowell, T. (1981). *Ethnic America.* New York: Basic Books.

Spann, E. (1981). *New Metropolis, New York City, 1840–1857.* New York: Columbia University Press.

Steward, E. C. (1972). *American Cultural Patterns.* La Grange Park, IL: Intercultural Network.

Takaki, R. (1993). *A Different Mirror: A History of Multicultural America.* Boston: Little, Brown.

Trattner, W. (1974). *From Poor Law to Welfare State: A History of Social Welfare in America.* New York: Free Press.

Van den Berghe, P. (1981). *The Ethnic Phenomenon.* New York: Elsevier Science.

Warren, R. (1993). *Estimates of the Resident Illegal Alien Population: October, 1992.* Washington, DC: U.S. Immigration and Naturalization Service.

Weber, M. (1961). Ethnic groups. In T. Parsons (Ed.), *Theories of Society.* New York: Free Press.

Williams, L. (1988). Frameworks for introducing racial and ethnic minority content into the curriculum. In C. Jacobs and D. Bowles (Eds.), *Ethnicity and Race: Critical Concepts in Social Work* (pp. 167–184). Silver Spring, MD: National Association of Social Workers.

2

Ethnicity and Social Work Practice with Individuals

A great deal of social work practice, perhaps the major part if one were to look at how social workers actually spend their time, is devoted to working with and on behalf of individual clients. Pointing out this fact does not gainsay the importance of social work practice with collectivities such as groups, families, organizations, and communities. Social workers do and should work in the fields of policy analysis and development, administration, and research, as teachers and consultants, and in many other professional roles. Yet working directly with an individual client in order to help that person address an identified need, and to fulfill one of the purposes of social work practice—prevention, provision of resources, and rehabilitation (Boehm, 1959)—remains at the core of the profession.

Before proceeding, it may be useful to look at what we mean by the term *individual.* Most social work theorists distinguish clearly between their definitions of *individuals* and *social systems.* A typical definition of social system is

> an identifiable unit of two or more persons who interact in such a way that change in one or more such persons initiates change in other persons and this change, in turn, produces change in the persons with whom the interaction began. The interactions affect the whole unit as well as its parts. (Garvin and Seabury, 1984, p.11)

From other perspectives, however, the distinction between individual and system is neither clear nor distinct. Longres points out that, from both social system and ecological perspectives, a single human being can be thought of as a system: a series of subsystems or parts faced with the requirements all systems face if they are to survive (1995, pp. 21–31). Falck (1988), as noted elsewhere in this book (see chapter 3), considers the dichotomy between individual and group to be a false one. He has also written about the "seen" and "unseen" group in work with individuals. Greene (1991) points out that systems theory influenced the way in which the profession defined a "case" or a "client."

The case may be defined as a person, a family, a hospital ward, a housing complex, a particular neighborhood, a school population, a group with particular problems and needs, or a community with common concerns. The drawing of a systems boundary rather than a linear one provides for the true psychosocial perception of a case, because it includes the significant inputs into the lives of the individuals involved.This broader definition of a case allows the social worker to better decide what is the target of change—the individual, or client; the family, or larger system; or both—or whether it is appropriate to intervene at all (Greene, 1991).

There is a considerable body of opinion, then, that points to the complexity of the concept *individual client*. The same writers cited as dichotomizing individuals and systems themselves proceed to characterize "individual personality" as an empirical, organic *system* (Garvin and Seabury, 1984, p. 39).

This discussion may strike the reader as slightly esoteric. At least some writers think that one can view individuals as systems. There is some agreement that establishing the boundary for the "client-system" (Pincus and Minahan, 1973) is not necessarily simple. What has this to do with ethnicity and with social work practice with individuals? It is useful to think about the various ways in which "individual client" can be defined for at least three reasons.

First, when a client comes to a social worker for help, or is coerced into coming, since a significant proportion of clients come involuntarily (Northen, 1995, pp. 216–217), one may view the situation as much more complex than the meeting of two people. Both client and worker may be viewed as systems in the sense sketched above. And each may be viewed as a part—the tips of their respective icebergs, as it were—of complex systems. The worker brings to an interview membership in an agency or other organizational auspice, the social work profession and, last but not least, both gender and ethnic identities. The client brings family, group and community memberships, self-assessment of strengths and weaknesses, and ethnic identity in interaction with gender identity.

Coming to a social worker, whether voluntarily or not, constitutes asking for help. As will be seen, various aspects of coming for and receiving help are differently defined, perceived, and evaluated within various ethnic communities. Ethnocultural definitions and norms affect, at a minimum:

1. The kinds of circumstances an individual should be able to deal with without getting help from others.
2. The kinds of problems and situations entitle one to seek help from one's family.
3. The circumstances that "justify" seeking help from a professional, a person who may or may not share an ethnic identity with the applicant.
4. What constitutes help.
5. Who is party to and involved in the helping process, for example, the client's family, colleagues, neighbors, and employer.
6. Potential or actual stigmas associated with asking for and getting help, and how to best neutralize them.
7. The obligations imposed, by the nature of the helping process, upon worker and client, and the client's family and community, respectively.

Other aspects of the social work process that may be affected by viewing the individual as a system include the question of confidentiality. With whom is a worker dealing or, phrased differently, who is the client? This issue can become particularly telling when family or community members involve themselves or seek to involve themselves with a social worker around the helping process with a member of their family or community.

All of this is not to imply, of course, that all members of a given ethnic community will bring the same expectations or experience a helping relationship identically, but rather that there are some patterned regularities roughly correlated with membership in particular ethnic communities and with having internalized the norms and values of an ethnic culture. These regularities affect the ethnic lens of the client.

The Nature of the Social Work Process: Client and Worker Roles

Mutual Expectations

For a helping process to take place for a social work client, a bond or relationship must develop between client and worker. In one conceptual framework, the applicant for service needs to go through a process of role induction in order to become a client and benefit from help (Perlman, 1957). The relationship between client and worker may range from the purely instrumental on the one hand, to one within which a client experiences, reexperiences, or expresses the most intense and intimate feelings. Nor is the social worker a passive element in the helping process. The worker carries responsibility for conscious use of self, maintaining self-discipline, setting limits, and establishing boundaries throughout the process. Nonetheless, the worker is a participant in a relationship process and, as such, is affected by the helping relationship and its outcomes.

There is no aspect of the helping process, nor of social work with individuals *in toto*, which is unique to work with people of one ethnic identity or another. Rather, it is our position that each and every aspect of social work practice is affected by the ethnic identity of the client (to say nothing of the worker), and by aspects of ethnic cultures which accompany a client, symbolically if not physically, to the worker's office or wherever the social worker's services are provided.

> Even voluntary clients have ambivalent feelings about applying for a service. They almost always have anxieties about a new experience; they have no way of knowing how they will be received and what will happen to them; they are hesitant about their own abilities to meet the practitioner's expectations. There is a sense of stigma attached to certain types of problems, such as a man's inability to provide for his family, certain illnesses such as epilepsy and AIDS, and such behavior as child neglect and spouse abuse. The still prevalent ethic in America that people should be independent and pull themselves up by their bootstraps makes it difficult to admit a need for help. In some cultures, the preference is for solving problems within the family. (Northen, 1995, p. 217)

There may be several reasons why asking for help is difficult for a member of a minority ethnic community. A client's lack of comfortable fluency in English and ignorance of other languages by a social worker can combine to make communication difficult. Communication in a social work interview often depends upon nuance as well as words, and on communicating feelings as well as objective facts.

Many immigrants come from societies in which encounters with "officials" lead to no good and in which voluntary, nongovernmental helping agencies are rare or unknown. Members of ethnic or racial communities that have been the objects of bigotry, oppression, and discrimination may simply mistrust social workers and social agencies, identifying them with the historical hurt and injustice inflicted on their communities. As a result, children may be socialized not to share "our" secrets with "them," or "not to wash dirty linen in public," or not to "disgrace the race." All of these teach that one does not go outside ethnic boundaries to discuss problems. All that happens if one does is that one is misunderstood and one's family gets into trouble.

Matching Clients and Workers

The question of the importance of matching clients and workers is one that needs much further study. Tolson (1988), reviewing research with regard to matching on gender, race, and class, concludes that little is known. Webb (1983), in a review of research on matching, did not find firm agreement. Davis and Proctor (1989) point out that, without question, for the foreseeable future, many clients of color will be receiving services from white social workers.

The effectiveness of nonethnic social workers with ethnic populations depends to a large part on their ability to understand the ethnic community and to offer services that are both responsive and responsible to the culture of the specific group (Gutierrez and Ortega, 1991). Green's (1995) ethnic competence model for practice rests upon a knowledge base that begins by identifying what is salient in the client's culture for the problems that are commonly brought to the worker. But the interpretation of saliency is itself a complex process involving, in addition to a basic knowledge of the culture, working with and learning from others who are culturally different. Previous experiences with others of the same ethnicity as the social worker will affect an applicant's reaction. Perhaps the biggest mistake one can make is to pretend that the differences between client and worker do not exist (Pinderhughes, 1989).

Nonethnic workers often find that they need a translator to work with a client who is not fluent in English. However, the translator is a third person introduced into the client-worker relationship, and this can affect the candor of the client's responses. Depending on the relationship of the interpreter to the client, the client may be reluctant to discuss behaviors or problems that could be interpreted negatively. If a translator is necessary, intrusiveness can be reduced by taking specific cautions. Guidelines for working with a translator include assuring that the person is trained; making sure to speak to the client, not the translator; discussing the meaning of terms; frequently repeating and summarizing; keeping the agenda short; allowing extra time; and writing a summary after the interview (Lee, 1988).

People are diverse in several ways, along several dimensions. This multiplicity of identities raises complications regarding matching workers and clients, even where the logistics and resources of the situation allow for such matches. Is it more important, for example, to match clients with workers of similar ethnic backgrounds or of roughly comparable ages? What about sexual orientations? Gender? Social class backgrounds and life experiences? Illnesses? The number of variables on which clients and workers can be matched quickly becomes unmanageable, in our view. There may well be instances in which matching a particular client to a particular worker makes sense and is feasible. There will be many situations in which it is impracticable and the variable along which matching should take place is unknown.

Hurdle (1990) underscores the importance of an ethnic-sensitive approach to practice based on a dual perspective that is aware that ethnic clients live in two worlds, that of the dominant culture and that of a unique cultural community. Consequently, the primary role of practitioners is to assist clients and services in bridging the gap between these worlds.

Feelings and Perceptions

Several writers (e.g., Shulman, 1992) use the phrase "tuning in" to identify a process of developing trusting communication and accurate mutual perceptions between client and social worker. Following this radio metaphor, it is important to recognize that client and worker need to "get on the same wavelength" with regard to several aspects of the helping process. These include feelings toward each other such as the boundaries within which feelings may be expressed or acted upon. The socialization of emotions takes place within an ethnic environment. When the client and the worker are unaware of their own lenses or of each other's, accurate communication becomes difficult or impossible. Sooner or later, both client and worker will perceive the other as someone from whom to flee, rather than someone to approach.

Another element that combines both feeling and perception pertains to the matter of trust. Trust in a social work relationship is both important and multifaceted. Two aspects should be highlighted. One is trust in the ethics, boundaries, and limits of the relationship. The process of coming for help involves the sense that one is entrusting parts of one's being to another person, something that is difficult enough if the other person is trustworthy but is impossible if the other is not. Issues for the client may range from the distinction between a personal and professional relationship to the fear, regrettably sometimes justified, of exploitation at a time of vulnerability and need.

Another trust issue revolves around comfort with and belief in the competence of the helper. Middle-class clients generally have a choice of social workers or other sources of help. Poor clients very often do not. One has little choice as to whether or not to seek help if the help includes needed concrete services or resources, or if seeking help is mandated as, for example, by a court.

In a brilliant series of studies done in the 1950s but relevant today, Polansky and Kounin studied what they called "the expected behaviors of potentially helpful persons" (1956). Their findings identified two sets of concerns on the part of a person coming for help. Does the potential helper *care* about me and my problem(s)? Does the potential helper *have knowledge and resources* to help me with my problem(s)? Clearly, an applicant has to make these judgments largely on the basis of affective factors, nonverbal and verbal cues, and emotional reactions to initial contacts with a social worker. There are also cognitive components to the judgments, and we shall discuss these next. But with regard to the affective components, the feelings—the sense that one will be understood, helped, and empathized with; that one has come to the "right place" and to the "right person,"—ethnic lenses and what they transmit play an important part.

One should not be simplistic about the ways in which ethnoracial identities operate and emotional messages ("vibes," if one prefers) are transmitted, received, and interpreted. As discussed, there is not simply desire to get help from a social worker who has the same ethnic heritage as the client. Rather, there is evidence that there are a series of questions, overt and covert, in the mind of a person who meets for the first time with a social worker in a professional relationship.

Somewhere in the process of building a relationship of trust is a question, often in the past unspoken, not only about whether the social worker likes, understands, and empathizes with *me* (the individual client) but also about how the social worker feels about and perceives *us* (my ethnoracial group). Is the social worker prejudiced against us? Does the social worker reveal this by inept or even offensive discussion about us? By insensitive jokes and evident discomfort? By the use of stereotyped assumptions in asking questions? In short, is the mix of my ethnoracial (or religious, regional, or other) identity and the social worker's going to be problematic?

In sum, then, the affective issues have to do with the perceived stance of the social worker with regard to the issues of importance to members of an ethnic community. As we shall see in chapters 6 and 7, each service system is also perceived as having a position, being in sympathy with or contemptuous of the values and standards of the community. Such perceptions, accurate or not, once formed, are hard to change.

Social workers and their organizations can be perceived as vehicles for empowerment, enabling members of the community to take greater control of life and its institutions (Lum, 1992; Pinderhughes, 1989; Solomon, 1976). Or, they may be perceived at the opposite pole, as agents of what Garvin and Seabury, following Blauner, call "internal colonialism" (1984, p. 327). The lens through which agencies and other institutions are viewed as a colonialist perceives them as a part of the structure of oppression and control that breaks down the structures, values, and social patterns of an ethnic community.

Cognitive and Methodological Elements

One of the requirements of a helping relationship is that each person accurately perceive the other, the other's role, the nature of the situation, and the mutual expectations. The "contract" between client and worker needs to be understood accurately by both, and should be open to renegotiation as the situation progresses and changes. If worker or client perceives the situation one way and the other another, little effective help is likely to result. Feelings and cognitions are closely related, of course. What one understands, or does not, markedly affects how one feels. And how one feels, or does not, markedly affects what one can perceive and what one can learn.

Cognitive processes are directly affected by ethnoracial identity and by past experiences with others of the same and of different identities. These experiences may be personal, or may have happened to others of the community and been absorbed into the mythic structure which all ethnic groups preserve and transmit to their members. Perception and feelings intertwine when it comes to what a social worker is "after," what the worker is "trying to do," what social workers "are good for" and are not.

Let us turn to a specific example. With surprisingly few exceptions, the traditional stance for social workers to take with individual clients has been for the worker to be quite opaque, unrevealing, and mysterious, on the one hand, and relatively noninteractive, on the other. For fairness, we should point out that some of the exceptions are important and include authoritative casework under the auspices of protective services, court-mandated services, work with chemically dependent people, and many forms of residential treatment. Even in these fields of practice, in which the traditional, noninteractive, reflective styles and stances are clearly not appropriate, professional behavior has generally been viewed as ruling out transparency and self-revelation beyond the most basic facts.

Relatively little attention has been paid to the fact that these prescriptions for professional behavior are based on experience with one race, largely with one class, at one time in history, and in certain particular parts of Europe. By breaking the rules of polite social interaction at that time and place, first psychoanalysis and then related forms of psychotherapy made distinct contributions to practice in various fields, not the least of them social work.

What was missing was an awareness that, to many members of various ethnic backgrounds, the traditional professional role behaviors were and are outside the bounds of the appropriate. The forms of interaction involved were outside the experience of many potential clients. For example, asking a question did not necessarily lead to the kind of response expected. Often this pattern resulted in discontinuance of participation on the client's part, and just as often the reason for the discontinuance was that the social worker was not relevant, interested, or able to help "people like us."

Again, we urge the reader not to overgeneralize or stereotype. Members of various minority groups do, indeed, value a reflective stance, and may experience as empowering a reluctance by practitioners to tell clients what to do. In many instances, however, a lack of interactivity—not answering when asked a question, not responding with relevant information when asked about oneself—is perceived as rejection or as judgmental. This erects barriers between worker and client and is not experienced by the client as help.

We do not advocate "letting it all hang out" and abandoning professional discipline. What we urge is an ongoing awareness of the ways in which ethnic clients perceive and experience stances and styles which workers adopt. Flexibility and an ability to adapt one's personal style to the expectations of clients are both essential for effective helping.

Various studies have identified the components of effective counseling. Among those mentioned most often are Truax and Carkhuff's listing of genuineness, accurate emphathy, and nonpossessive warmth (1967). Our position is that one needs to understand ethnic and cultural variations in experiencing these qualities. To return to our example, a refusal to interact verbally in a full and balanced manner is often experienced as rejection and as a statement that the social worker does not consider the client "worthy." This may be especially true when the client is not a native English speaker, or is an immigrant, but examples can also be found from worker-client transactions where both are native English speakers.

Behavioral Aspects

Effective social work practice with individual clients requires an understanding of the meanings of various worker and client behaviors experienced through various ethnic lenses. Specific behaviors, as well as patterns of relationship formation, have a great deal of meaning in working with individuals. Ethnic lenses color both. Here are some simple examples:

- Shaking hands firmly while looking the other person in the eye has considerable meaning for most of American society. The act of shaking hands, however, may have much different meanings for clients socialized in other cultures or members of particular ethnocultural groups. Looking someone directly in the eye may be defined as intrusive, especially if the looker is younger than the person looked at. Touch may violate taboos if the two people involved are adults of opposite sex, are of different ages, and the touch does not go in the direction of older-to-younger.
- Refusal by the social worker to respond to a direct question about one's family, or whether one has children, for example, may be perceived by the client as rejection rather than professional discipline.
- Specific words or topics may have particular meanings, negative or positive. An example of the latter is characterizing a client as a parent. Emphasizing motherhood or fatherhood carries a positive connotation and connotes prestige and status in many, if not all, ethnic cultures.
- On the other hand, a direct discussion of sexual behaviors may be viewed as highly intrusive, even dangerous, depending on the respective sexes and ethnic identities of worker and client.
- There is great cultural variation about what is appropriate and inappropriate to discuss at which stages of a relationship. This sensitivity often applies to the use of specific words. Members of many ethnic groups are particularly sensitive to whether or not the name of one's group or the client's own name is pronounced correctly. The worker's discomfort with learning or using a client's name is often equated by the client with devaluation.
- An important issue is that of timing. Americans are often viewed as crude or uncivilized because of their desire to "get down to business" as quickly as possible. Our culture values saving time. Many others value a sense of pace, inquiring as to the welfare and health of the other and their family. Failure to do so marks one participant as an uncaring worker and the other as an uncared for client.
- The need for pacing and relationship building sometimes conflicts with the rushed and sometimes disorderly realities of agencies in the age of budget cuts and limited resources. A client may expect 10 to 15 minutes of general conversation as a polite introduction to an extended conversation. A worker in, say, a health care setting, may only have 10 to 15 minutes altogether to spend with the client. There is value to sharing realistic time constraints. We should be aware, however, that the perception that "the social worker is always busy when I come in" is a significant negative element for many ethnic clients. The opposite is also true.

- Being on time for appointments is another area in which conflict and misunderstandings can occur. The often strict adherence of professionals to punctuality may not be shared by ethnic clients who perceive the relationship itself as most important. Being 20 minutes late can easily be perceived by a social worker as a sign of indifference or lack of motivation, while for the client it is normative behavior. Frustration or anger on the part of the social worker can easily be misinterpreted by a client, affecting the helping relationship negatively.

Overcoming Communication Barriers

Effective social work practice requires a career-long commitment to developing, refining, and updating cultural competence (Chau, 1990; Comas-Diaz, 1988; Davis and Proctor, 1989; Hurdle, 1990; Nakanishi and Rittner, 1992). We view acquiring such competence as a process which requires an ongoing commitment both to learn about other ethnocultural groups and to stay in touch with one's own ethnic identity. As Lewin (1951) and many others point out, it is hardly rewarding to relate to others' identities while being ambivalent about one's own. Learning about ethnocultural differences, patterns, activities, schools, foods, holidays, family patterns, beliefs, and practices about child rearing and caring for older people can be enriching for social workers, personally as well as professionally.

The sheer multiplicity of ethnic groups in our society makes it impossible for any social worker to be expert about all of them. As an indicator of the diversity of contemporary American society, the social work staff of one Maryland county department of social services reported that members of 27 defined ethnic groups were represented within the agency's caseload. The headmaster of one well-known Massachusetts high school reported that a total of 17 different languages were spoken as primary languages in the homes of students at his one school.

Partly for this reason, we recommend that social workers *encourage clients to be their teachers* when it comes to learning about ethnocultural patterns, patterns of perception and ways of perceiving the life cycle, beliefs about family processes and norms, and beliefs about asking for and receiving help. There are several advantages to taking a learning stance as a social worker:

1. It enables social workers to learn and to increase our understanding of ethnocultural patterns.

2. It serves to equalize, to an extent, the unequal power relationships inherent in the client-worker interaction. The majority of such interactions take place on the social worker's turf, in a situation in which the client hurts while the social worker does not, where a social worker is often the one with either the symbolic or the real keys and the client is not. Putting the client in the teacher's chair, even if only temporarily, can be empowering to the client.
3. The expression of genuine interest in learning from the client is an appropriate and sometimes facilitating step in developing a relationship of mutual respect, trust, and shared responsibility for the helping process.
4. Such interaction can also provide important cues and clues for assessment by the worker and self-assessment by the client.

We repeat our earlier caution about stereotyping. Minority ethnic groups in our society range from tens of thousands to tens of millions. It is foolish to talk about "how African Americans look at families" or "how Latinos look at the life cycle," or "how Asian Americans view the helping process." It is wise and, we think, always appropriate to ask a client how she or he, as an ethnic group member *and as a person*, views any of these. It is also appropriate, generally, to ask how something is or was viewed *in a client's family*. The question can sometimes be asked, "How were you brought up to think of [for example] asking for help?"

Despite one's best efforts, the situation will arise, sooner or later, in which practitioners will say or do something that will offend a client. One should be sensitive to evidence that this has happened. An appropriate response, in our view, is to apologize, give the client a chance to respond, and move on. Social workers are not expected to be perfect, but rather to model appropriate behaviors at times of imperfect behavior.

Next, let us take a look at specific phases and processes of clinical practice with individuals and ways in which some of the principles sketched so far in the chapter can be applied.

Assessment

Lum (1992) points out that

> assessment, in social work practice, is an in-depth investigation of the psychosocial dynamics that affect the client and the client's environment. . . . Assessment of ethnic-minority clients identifies positive cultural strengths in the client's ethnic background. It moves away from a pathological investi-

> gation, which tends to evaluate internal and external liabilities. . . . Ethnic-oriented assessment should strive for a psychosocial balance between objective external factors of the community and subjective internal reactions. Ethnic beliefs, family solidarity, community support networks and other cultural assets are intervening variables. (p. 167)

In Lum's view, as in many others (Chunn, Dunston, and Ross-Sheriff, 1983; Davis and Proctor, 1989; Devore and Schlesinger, 1994; Ho, 1975; Lefley, 1986; Lewis and Ho, 1975; Pinderhughes, 1989; Proctor and Davis, 1994; Solomon, 1976; Staples, 1981, 1988; Sue and McKinney, 1975), assessment of members of ethnic communities needs to be done from several perspectives. Chief among them is an understanding of the nature of behavior patterns, norms, and survival strategies in ethnic communities, particularly within a historical pattern of oppression that may stretch over two continents, in the case of immigrants, or over centuries, in the case of African Americans.

It is our contention that the past 30 years have seen massive changes in the ways in which ethnicity is viewed within the social work profession. These changes, brought about partly because of greater awareness of ethnic diversity, partly beause of pressures brought to bear by ethnic professionals, and partly because of greater awareness of psychosocial linkages, have had many outcomes, some to be welcomed and some to be questioned.

It is clear that social workers need to be educated and prepared to understand the meanings of behaviors within an ethnic community context. The repeated advice in the *Diagnostic and Statistical Manual of Mental Disorders-IV* (*DSM-IV*, American Psychiatric Association, 1994) that the clinician take into account the person's community context and cultural norms before making a diagnosis is one example of an advance we welcome. More remains to be done, of course. We view ethnic identity as a powerful influence on the behavior of all who are members of ethnic groups and communities.

Behaviors that could be characterized as pathological, such as viewing a social worker with great suspicion at a first meeting, may be adaptive and quite comprehensible when displayed by a person who has been denied rights or has been the victim of hate violence (Barnes and Ephross, 1995). Social stressors are often intense in minority communities, and people under stress behave in ways that have different meanings that need to be understood. Ethnic clients, in particular, need to be listened to carefully as they define from their perspective the problems they face. Social workers need to be careful, indeed, before assuming a stance that we know better than the client what the client needs.

At the same time, we are concerned that genuine and painful self-destructive pathologies not be concealed beneath a cloak of ethnic diversity. A simple theory of social causation can blind a worker to prorlems that can be solved and pathology that can be treated.

Effective assessment in social work practice requires balance and joint participation of client and worker to the maximum feasible point, empathic awareness of cultural differences, and the best, most trusting, communication possible. No one of these elements substitutes for another. Using the assumed or supposed characteristics of an ethnic group to solve a worker's own identity confusions or to express a worker's resentments against the majority culture can be harmful to ethnically identified clients. Lum points out the dangers of stereotpying in both directions: stereotyping against the minority ethnic culture and overidentification with its real or supposed virtues (1992).

Contracting and the Structure of Service

Contracting is a process of reaching agreement between client and worker as to the nature, objectives, limits, terms, and timing of social work help. Effective contracting for services requires two things: accurate and consensual problem identification and clear and consistent two-way communication between client and worker. It requires an awareness of the lenses of worker and client and a strong attempt to get a clear field of vision through both. This requires close attention, both when client and worker share an ethnic identity and when they do not. It is important that the worker be able to speak more than one language—in the first instance symbolically, in the second instance actually.

The social worker needs to be able to move readily back and forth between the professional language of problem identification and the terms and words used by the client, with accuracy and without condescension. Rather than assuming that the client, or the client's family, understand the methods, format, or jargon of clinical social work, for example, these should be spelled out and discussed. Operating within a rigid, once-a-week, 50-minute hour makes little sense to many people who are in crisis, especially to a member of an ethnic community for whom this pattern of use of time feels foreign.

The place of meeting often has considerable significance. At least one home visit may have great meaning to the client and may be a source of useful perspective for the social worker as well. Thus, it may be helpful both for assessment and for treatment, as well as for the contracting process. Unfortunately, being a social worker no longer surrounds one with an invisible shield against violence, as it may once have done. In some instances, however, unrealistic fears and media-generated stereotypes prevent social workers from making the obviously desirable home visit that was a standard part of social work practice in times past.

Language may pose another problem, serving as it does as an almost literal lens through which people perceive and understand each other. Often, someone who is speaking a second or third language is able to grasp the overt, symbolic content of a conversation better than the nuanced, more subtle qualities. Creativity, patience, and understanding are necessary to bridge language gaps. Family members—often children, who may be better skilled in English—can help by interpreting. Using family members in this way may necessitate some alteration of the usual standards of confidentiality, so it is important to make sure that the client understands and supports this alteration. In many instances, far from objecting to family members knowing what is going on, clients are reassured by being able to talk with a trusted family member about what is happening in the meetings with the social worker.

Defining Professional Relationships

The professional relationship, bounded by ethical standards, focused on the needs of the client rather than on those of the worker, voluntary on the part of the client, yet intimate and characterized by trust, is a complex cultural artifact. Though it shares certain things with other relationships with which the client may be familiar, such as relationships with a member of the clergy or a physician, it may also be unique in the experience of an ethnic client. It should not be taken for granted that the client understands the relationship. It deserves explanation and open discussion, again with patience and without condescension. No one is born, after all, understanding what there is to know about professional helping relationships.

Ethnic clients, as well as other clients, may assume that the relationship of intimacy and trust developed in client-worker interaction will carry over into outside life, with the worker becoming a sort of surrogate relative. The limits, as well as the potential, of the social worker–client relationship need to be discussed and spelled out with cl
tact, then reinforced periodically as needed during the cour
relationship.

Working Together

American social work's context includes the values of American society and culture. One of its important values is self-determination. However oppressed by deprivation, discrimination, or unjust social policies, Americans have traditionally valued personal freedom and abhorred coercion, at least for themselves. Though some have questioned the extent to which social work still values self-determination (e.g., Bernstein, 1993), it remains enshrined in the pantheon of social work values. It is important to remember that, while social work celebrates self-determination, the reality of this commitment is mistrusted in many communities.

Members of some communities know social workers as people who come to investigate you, recommend removing your children from your home, find you ineligible for benefits or services, or work with police departments perceived as oppressive and unjust. Members of such communities may be wary of working with a social worker. If the worker is perceived as an agent of an oppressive system—as a member of "them" rather than as one of "us"—one can hardly expect trust and openness. Nor can an individual social worker wipe out the perceptions of a community, however much one may want to do so.

The starting point needs to be acknowledgment of "where the client is," to use one of the oldest and most apt of social work concepts. An open discussion of how to get past barriers is far more likely to be successful than denial or defensiveness, and certainly more likely to be successful than retreating into hurt and feeling unappreciated on the part of the worker. This is one area in which workers need to be concerned with the clarity and focus of our own lenses, through which we understand our experiences as well as those of the client.

Termination

More attention has been paid in the social work literature to beginnings than to endings, to a first interview than to a last. Termination, with its emotional connotations of ending and death, is often a difficult experience for workers, as well as for clients. Its importance, though, can hardly be overstated, especially when a social worker has been of significant help to a client. Even more than some others, ethnically identified clients can resist and deny termination and experience it as rejection or as invalidating the progress that has come out of the entire experience. Persons accustomed to strong, informal ties may also perceive termination as invalidating the entire relationship experience with the worker.

It is all the more important that termination include discussion in considerable depth, not only at a feeling level but also with clear action guidelines. Will the worker be available to the client in the future in case of need? If not, who will be? Does the client know whom to call and how? Has the client met that person? Has there been some chance for discussion and for the by-now trusted and admired social worker to transfer some of the client's feelings to the staff and the agency in general? Will the social worker come to the client's child's graduation?

The guiding principle is never to promise what the worker will not carry out. In many ethnic communities, giving a professional who has been helpful a gift is simply a standard courtesy, and the gift should be treated in that way, if possible. Ceremonial endings help with termination and should not be treated as illegitimate by workers. It is often useful for workers to acknowledge that termination is difficult for them, too.

Working Through the Ethnic Lens

This chapter has examined the ways in which ethnicity can affect the relationship between a social worker and an ethnic client. Each aspect of this relationship, from the time of the first contact through termination, is perceived through an ethnic lens. Given the importance of these lenses for the development and maintenance of the relationship, it is essential to recognize how distortions in them, by either the client or the practitioner, can affect the helping process.

The social worker is responsible for having and using a lens that can view accurately both the expectations of the client with regard to help and the worker's role in offering this help. The lens through which the client is perceived must be sensitive to the specific traditions or values of the ethnic group, including but not limited to those that may cause clients to be reluctant or resistant to participating in the helping process. This sensitivity is a powerful and important tool for helping to clarify the ethnic lens of the client.

We have emphasized the importance of trust as a foundation to the relationship between social worker and client. Trust develops out of a sense of security and belief in the credibility of (understanding the legitimacy of) the other. Both the worker and the client are dependent upon a sense of trust, and this can only occur when each perceives the other through transparent and accurate lenses. For the worker this entails understanding that traditional professional roles and behaviors may be misunderstood by ethnic clients. Being aware of the ways in which they may be misinterpreted and helping the client to perceive them not as signs of rejection or indicators of an absence of caring are essential to the relationship.

We have emphasized that, as one works toward clarifying the ethnic lens, it is critical not to stereotype. All members of an ethnic group do not necessarily adhere to the same beliefs or expectations. The client is an *individual*, and it is crucial to understand the unique attitudes and views of the person with whom one is engaged and how they may deflect or differ from those of other members of the same ethnic group.

A Case for Discussion

Harold Lee was referred to the Family Center by Officer Carol Foote of the Claw County Police Department. Officer Foote had responded to a radio message phoned in to the department through the emergency help number 3 days before by Mrs. Sally Lee, who, like her husband, had been born in Korea and emigrated to the United States 5 years before. The two have three children, ages 4 to 9, and work together in a produce market owned by a relative of Mrs. Lee's. Mrs. Lee had called the emergency help line because her husband was threatening to beat her if she continued to meet her female friends for lunch on her day off. She said that she was occasionally beaten by her husband before they emigrated, but this had not happened since their arrival in the United States. Officer Foote had filled out a formal statement which would require Mr. Lee to appear in court, and suggested strongly that Mr. Lee seek evaluation and help at the Family Center.

Questions for Discussion

1. The authors state,"when a client comes to a social worker for help . . . one may view the situation as more complex than the meeting of two people." What does this statement mean? Can you illustrate, referring to a client with whom you have worked or are familiar?
2. Give an example of a situation in which the expectations of an ethnic client and a social worker may be dissonant. How may this dissonance be resolved?

3. Identify four aspects of a "contract" between a social worker and a client that are especially important when working with an ethnic client.
4. List five behaviors of social workers that may need to be modified in order to communicate effectively with members of a particular ethnic group.
5. Discuss the process of termination with a client. How may the ethnic identity of the client affect this process? What about the ethnic identity of the worker?

References

American Psychiatric Association. (1994). *Diagnostic and Statistical Manual of Mental Disorders* (4th ed.). Washington, DC: Author.

Barnes, A., and Ephross, P. H. (1995). The impact of hate crimes on victims: Emotional and behavioral responses to attacks. *Social Work 39*(3), 247–251.

Bernstein, S. (1993). Whatever happened to self-determination? In S. Wenocur, P. H. Ephross, T. V. Vassil, and R. V. Varghese (Eds.), *Group Work: Expanding Horizons* (pp. 3–14). Binghamton, NY: Haworth Press.

Boehm, W. (1959). The nature of social work, *Social Work, 3*(2), 10–18.

Chau, K. L. (Ed.) (1990). *Ethnicity and Biculturalism: Emerging Perspectives in Social Group Work.* Binghamton, NY: Haworth Press.

Chunn, J. C., Dunston, P. J., and Ross-Sheriff, F. (1983). *Mental Health and People of Color: Curriculum Development and Change.* Washington, DC: Howard University Press.

Comas-Diaz, L. (1988). *Cross-Cultural Mental Health Treatment.* New York: Wiley.

Davis, L. E., and Proctor, E. (1989). *Race, Gender and Class: Guidelines for Practice with Individuals, Families and Groups.* Boston: Allyn and Bacon.

Devore, W., and Schlesinger, E. (1994). *Ethnic-sensitive Social Work Practice*, (4th ed.). Boston: Allyn and Bacon.

Falck, H. S. (1988). *Social Work: The Membership Perspective.* New York: Springer.

Garvin, C. D., and Seabury, B. A. (1984). *Interpersonal Practice in Social Work: Processes and Procedures.* Englewood Cliffs, NJ: Prentice Hall.

Goffman, E. (1961). *Asylums: Essays on the Social Situation of Mental Patients and Other Inmates.* Garden City, NY: Doubleday.

Green, J. (1995). *Cultural Awareness in the Human Services* (2nd ed.). Englewood Cliffs, NJ: Prentice Hall.

Greene, R. R. (1991). General systems theory. In R. R. Greene and P. H. Ephross (Eds.), *Human Behavior Theory and Social Work Practice* (pp. 227–259). New York: Aldine de Gruyter.

Gutierrez, L., and Ortega, R. (1991). Developing methods to empower Latinos: The importance of groups, *Social Work with Groups, 14*(2), 23–43.

Ho, M. K. (1975). Social work with Asian-Americans. *Social Casework, 57*(3).

Hurdle, D. E. (1990). The ethnic group experience. In K. L. Chau (Ed.), *Ethnicity and Biculturalism: Emerging Perspectives in Social Group Work*. Binghamton, NY: Haworth Press.

Lee, E. (1988). Cultural factors in working with Southeast Asian refugee adolescents. *Journal of Adolescence, 11*, 167–169.

Lefley, H. P. (Ed.). (1986). *Cross-Cultural Training for Mental Health Professionals*. Springfield, IL: Charles C Thomas.

Lewin, K. (1951). In D. Cartwright (Ed.), *Field Theory in Social Science: Selected Theoretical Papers*. New York: Harper and Brothers.

Lewis, R. G., and Ho, M.K. (1975). Social work with Native Americans. *Social Work, 20*, 379–382.

Longres, J. F. (1995). *Human Behavior in the Social Environment* (2nd ed.). Itasca, IL: F. E. Peacock.

Lum, D. (1992). *Social Work Practice and People of Color: A Process-stage Approach* (2nd ed.). Monterey, CA: Brooks/Cole.

Nakanishi, M., and Rittner, B. (1992). The inclusionary cultural model. *Journal of Social Work Education, 28*(1), 27–35.

Northen, H. (1995). *Clinical Social Work Knowledge and Skills* (2nd ed.). New York: Columbia University Press.

Perlman, H. H. (1957). *Social Casework: A Problem-solving Process*. Chicago: University of Chicago Press.

Pincus, A., and Minahan, A. (1973). *Social Work Practice: Model and Method*. Itasca, IL: F. E. Peacock.

Pinderhughes, E. B. (1989). *Understanding Race, Ethnicity and Power*. New York: Macmillan.

Polansky, N., and Kounin, J. (1956). Client's reactions to initial interviews: A field study. *Human Relations, 9*, 237–264.

Proctor, E. K., and Davis, L. E. (1994). The challenge of racial difference: Skills for clinical practice. *Social Work, 39*, 314–323.

Shulman, L. (1992). *The Skills of Helping Individuals, Families and Groups* (3rd ed.) Itasca, IL: F. E. Peacock.

Solomon, B. B. (1976). *Black Empowerment: Social Work in Oppressed Communities*. New York: Columbia University Press.

Staples, R. (1981). *The World of Black Singles*. Westport, CT: Greenwood Press.

Staples, R. (1988). Race and marital status: An overview. In H. P. McAdoo (Ed.), *Black Families*. Beverly Hills, CA: Sage.

Sue, S., and McKinney, H. (1975). Asian Americans in the community mental health care system. *American Journal of Orthopsychiatry, 45*(2).

Tolson, E. R. (1988). *The Metamodel and Clinical Social Work*. New York: Columbia University Press.

Truax, C. B., and Carkhuff, R. R. (1967). *Toward Effective Counseling and Psychotherapy*. Chicago: Aldine.

Webb, J. DeH. (1983). *The Effect of Therapist-Patient Compatibility upon Outcomes of Psychotherapy: A Field Study*. Unpublished doctoral dissertation, University of Maryland Graduate School, Baltimore.

3

Ethnicity and Social Work with Groups

There is an obvious consonance between the essence of ethnic identity and the conceptual definition of a group. Each revolves around the idea of a central theme in social work practice (Falck,1988), and each denotes a system with boundaries. Each involves a distinction between those who are and those are not "members," between those perceived and experienced as "us" and those perceived and experienced as "them," not "us." This distinction may be based on ancestry, in the case of ethnicity, or upon much less lasting characteristics, as in the case of a small group. The distinction is crucial, however. For without "them" there are no boundaries to "us." Without people who are not group members, the concept of group membership lacks meaning.

Students of ethnicity and social workers who work with groups may use the term *group* in two different senses. Social workers generally use a definition like that proposed by Bertcher (1994):

> A group is a dynamic social entity composed of two or more individuals. These individuals interact interdependently to achieve one or more common goals for the group or similar individual goals that each member believes can best be achieved through group participation. As a result of this participation, each member Influences and is influenced by every other member to some degree. Over time, statuses and roles develop for members, while norms and values that regulate behavior of consequence to the group are accepted by members. (p. 3)

Bertcher goes on to note, "[o]ne thing that makes this definition so interesting pertains to the phrase, 'over time' " (p. 3). Another is the fundamental importance of "group participation," which traditionally has required face-to-face interaction in small groups.

Clearly, the term *ethnic group* differs from Bertcher's definition. It is not conceivable that, say, all African Americans in Maryland or all Italian Americans in Michigan could interact face-to-face and affect each other in the ways that Bertcher spells out. Ethnic group membership is a symbolic identification, whether entered into voluntarily by an individual, assigned by the broader society on the basis of actual or presumed characteristics, or a combination of the two.

The Universality of Groups

Human beings are born into groups, survive and learn to relate to their physical and social environments as a result of learning in groups, grow to define themselves as members of some groups and not of others, and express themselves in and as members of groups. With very few exceptions, people die with their group identities intact; when they do, their physical remains are disposed of and their personal identities are mourned in and through group processes and structures maintained by their fellow members. To be human is to be a member of many groups, and stages of the human life cycle are marked by events given meaning by the participation in groups.

In modern Western thinking, it has been fashionable to think in terms of dualisms. Mind and body, for example, may be contrasted, even though they are clearly linked in a systemic relationship. Similarly, some contrast "individual" and "group" as though these represented polar opposites or, at least contrasting aspects of self. It has also become fashionable to view body and mind, social participation and psychological identity, as dimorphisms and dualities. In fact, it is difficult to think of human beings without viewing them as members of groups. We do not view the concepts of individual and group as opposites but as complementary: individuality is defined in large part by membership in groups, and membership is defined in large part by the fact that a group member is "a psychological being capable of private experience (Falck, 1988, p. 30). At the same time, small groups have been viewed as *microcosms*, literally "small worlds" (Ephross and Vassil, 1988).

One can be a member of many small groups simultaneously, and experience the joys of living in several microcosms. It is harder and less usual for an individual or family to be members of more than one ethnic group, though this certainly does happen.

Example

(Setting: a university faculty member's office)

"I didn't know Jacob is Latino. I thought he was Jewish."

> "You're right, he is."
> "I didn't know you could be both."
> "Of course you can. There are more than 400,000 Jews in Argentina."

The texture of life in ethnic groups, as in all human society, is given shape and meaning by membership in and the lives of small groups. The processes, structures, and experiences common to all small groups loom much larger than the differences, though various norms of small-group behavior are defined by ethnic identities and patterns.

Social workers work with groups of various types toward various ends. Desirable group outcomes sought by social workers include "growth, healing, expanded and enhanced social functioning, learning, the expression of democratic citizenship, the practice of self-determination, mutual aid, mutual support and progress toward achieving social justice" (Toseland and Rivas, 1995, pp. 20–45). Administrative groups add other *desiderata* such as effective management, efficient delivery of services, participatory decision making and increased levels of satisfaction for all levels of organizational participants (Brown, 1991). Various kinds of small groups, including but never limited just to families, exist in all known human societies and, therefore, in *all known* cultures. This is not to say that all cultures and people of all ethnic backgrounds approach small-group participation in the same way. The lenses through which groups are perceived, experienced, and evaluated differ considerably from one ethnic group to another, to say nothing of variance within ethnic groups. This latter variance may be age- or social-classed, or both, or subculturally based. It may correlate with community (e.g., rural, suburban, urban, metropolitan), or ancestry (old residents, newcomers; powerful family, low-power family), or other variables existing within a given society.

Depending on the purposes for which a group is formed, a social worker may want to help a group challenge traditional ethnic norms of group behavior or conform to them. In all instances, though, the worker needs to understand the ethnic patterns and their interrelationships. By knowledge and understanding, we are not referring here simply to cognitive or intellectual knowledge. Whether to help groups conform or challenge, the worker needs an inner sense of the emotions raised for group members by conforming to what may be centuries-old ethnic traditions, or modifying nonconforming behavior in groups, respectively. Nonconforming behavior may risk the charge of disloyalty, of being insufficiently ethnic, of being a turncoat. Terms such as "oreo" (they are white on the inside, though dark brown on the outside), "banana" (yellow on the outside but much whiter on the inside), or their equivalents carry deeply felt symbolic stigma for individuals and for groups. At an age at which the approval of peers is experienced as vital—adolescence, for example—the fear of such negative labels from one's own group can lead to exaggerated behaviors including but not limited to those destructive to self and to society.

Ethnicity and Variables in Group Structure and Process

What difference does ethnicity make in groups' lives? And what difference can or does or should members' ethnicity make for the professional role behaviors of social workers seeking to influence the experience of members in groups? Some writers analyze group life by using structure and process as analytic concepts (Ephross and Vassil, 1988). In this view, structure constitutes the relatively enduring aspects of group life, while process represents the moment-to-moment, more temporary aspects of what takes place in a group.

Other writers label differently the concepts they use to analyze what takes place in a group. Gitterman and Shulman (1994), referring primarily to treatment groups, list nine mutual aid processes: sharing data, the dialectical process, entering taboo areas, the all-in-the-same-boat phenomenon, mutual support, mutual demand, individual problem solving, rehearsal, and the strength-in-numbers phenomenon. Another list includes "goal determination, goal pursuit, [the development of] values and norms, role differentiation, communication-interaction, conflict resolution and behavior control, [changes in] emotions, group culture, group resources, extra group transactions, group boundaries and group climate" (Garvin, 1987, pp. 113–121).

Yet another list of group structures and processes highlights group composition and criteria for membership; some level of consensus on group goals; the eternal structure, which consists of time, space, and size; time, or the time framework within which the group meets; space; size; internal structure; cohesion; communication and decision making; norms, values and group culture, and group control and influence (Henry, 1992).

What difference does ethnic identity make? Every one of the variables previously listed is perceived, experienced, defined, and judged as desirable or not; each group experience is categorized through the lens constructed by ethnic identity as successful and rewarding or unsuccessful, stigmatizing, and frustrating. As noted, by no means does each member of an ethnic group, each sharer of ethnicity, respond identically or even similarly. Rather, the ethnic identity of group members, and the mix and proportion of ethnicity within a given group, are part of the experience of each member and therefore of the group as a whole.

How does ethnicity affect group life in ways of which social workers should be acutely aware? The following discussion is meant to be suggestive only and is offered in the hope that it will stimulate each social worker to think of other ways.

Groups are, in the final analysis, symbolic entities. Cohesion, affiliation, stages of group development, affective bonding, investment in the group-as-a-whole—all of these and many other dimensions of group life are symbolic qualities, given life and meaning by a consensus of meanings on the part of the group members. Symbolic interactionism, the theory of social life which is perhaps best suited to understanding small groups, emphasizes the importance of shared symbolic constructs, especially shared meanings of words and of language in general. A major part of ethnic identity is precisely the shared vocabulary of concepts, words, and symbols unique to people who share that identity. Ethnic identity is generally (not always, to be sure) accompanied by sharing in a language and a set of cultural traditions.

The accomplishment of some considerable degree of intimacy is characteristic of the development of a group. Regardless of the terms used, there is universal agreement among group theorists and practitioners that reaching an appropriate stage of intimacy and developing the trust that underlies and is prerequisite for intimacy are both essential if a group is truly to form. Intimacy, however, is defined differently and allowed differently by various ethnic traditions. Furthermore, there may be severe limitations on intimacy and its expressions to one sex and not another, or between people of one age group but not another, and so forth.

Example

> Jeremy, a young, energetic, highly regarded staff member, was frustrated by his apparent lack of success working with a group of recently arrived Vietnamese immigrant men. It took several weeks before the neighborhood center's program director could get some answers in informal discussion with two of the group's members. The group members said that "Mr. Jeremy," whom they both characterized as "well-meaning" was fond of making sexually tinged remarks and jokes. He also wore a small earring in his left ear. Also, he never wore a jacket to group meetings, even though the group members generally did. The program director suggested the group members

> confront Jeremy with these reactions. They refused and were so embarrassed by their refusal that they sought reassurance that they had the right to refuse. The two group members next asked the program director to talk with Mr. Jeremy. He suggested that he would be willing to mediate at an informal meeting. This strategy succeeded in opening channels of communication, though the meeting was a difficult one for all concerned. It was at the end of this meeting that the group agreed that, henceforth, members and worker should call each other by their first names.

Different levels of intimacy may be normative, expected, and therefore appropriate among people of the same ethnic group, but not when a group's membership is ethnically diverse. The same is true, we suggest, in groups composed of members of one sex, in contrast to those which are sexually mixed. In this sense, it may be appropriate to argue that the two sexes tend to treat each other as though they were two ethnic groups, to view each other with the same level of suspicion as one expects from people of different ethnicity who do not know each other well, and to attribute differences in behavior, attitude, and perception to sexual identity.

A social worker in a group may be of the same or different ethnic identity than the group members. Each has positive and negative aspects. Much depends upon the valuation that group members and worker put upon similarity and differences, respectively. Much also depends upon the worker's communication of his or her own similarity or difference with regard to the group members.

Levels of competitiveness, overt and covert, and the extent to which one is expected to submerge one's own needs to the welfare of the entire group, differ from one ethnic group to another. These differences mirror major historical differences that are embedded in and taught by various ethnic groups as part of their socialization of children and their induction of children into their ethnic identity. Group solidarity and emphasis on individual achievement, while not mutually exclusive, are valued differently by various ethnic groups. These values are taught to children by parents in a very direct and unapologetic way. Violating the historic norms is often perceived by parents as a rejection of themselves, while children and even adults who violate ethnic behavioral norms are often accused, with greater or lesser seriousness, of having become "one of them" rather than being or acting like "one of us."

Democracy and self-expression are not valued equally by people of varying ethnic backgrounds. These values, which underlie and are operationalized in the course of practicing group work, may be consonant with the values of an ethnic group and their culture, or they may be quite dissonant with these values. For example, social work with groups holds strongly to a view of healthy and responsible participation in which decision making allows, indeed requires, the active participation of each member, regardless of sex, age, or other personal characteristics.

We believe, together with the majority of the group workers of the Western world, that the microcosm of the small group should be a democratic one (Ephross and Vassil, 1988). This is not the view that people raised in many traditional cultures bring with them. For example, a person raised in a traditional, patriarchal culture may think it both proper and respectful to defer to the wishes of the worker, the "expert," rather than to listen to peers in the group who are little better off than himself or herself.

Nonverbal media have long been part of social work with groups. Recreational media such as games, sports, arts, crafts, dance, music, and drama were originally known as "program activities" or as just "program." They have been viewed by group workers as frameworks and tools for encouraging and guiding interactions within a group and sometimes between groups. Participation was also seen as having intrinsic benefits for group members, as were specific learnings brought about by group participation in particular activity media (see, e.g., Middleman, 1988).

Groups specifically designed for training and teaching, as well as some support and treatment groups, utilized some of the same activities and some different ones under the rubric of "experiential exercises." The term draws on the fact that group work derives much of its power to affect members' lives from the laboratory it offers, within which members can gain actual experience, can help themselves to obtain a social history, or can change and add to their old one. Members can try out and test new roles and interpersonal configurations and learn new ways of dealing with feelings, communicating, and responding, obtaining instant feedback from the other members and the worker.

Nonverbal activities are often utilized with groups whose members' ability to express themselves verbally is limited. Such groups range from those whose members are children, adolescents, or very old people to those who are coping in groups with crises, turmoil, or trauma in their lives. Other kinds of groups in which program activities are particularly useful include those whose members have diminished verbal capacities, such as groups for mentally retarded people, seriously mentally ill people, and hearing-impaired people.

In the context of our focus on ethnicity, it is interesting to note that program activities have often been employed, with great success, with groups composed of members who come from different cultures, speak different languages, or are recent immigrants. Activity media, however, carry important and sometimes intense meanings, culturally defined. Examples are not hard to find in American culture. Middle-aged and older women whose groups are dealing with preparing, serving, and eating food, even if it consists of very simple refreshments, often approach this activity with an intensity that makes it clear that their current and past roles as homemakers, feeders of their families, and food experts have profound meaning for their self-concepts and their self-esteem.

Despite the danger of stereotyping reactions, the same reaction can be seen in men of these ages whenever a group is faced with a problem which can be solved by either mechanical or construction expertise, to say nothing of matters automotive.

Example

> "Put your hands on the hips of the person in front of you" is an instruction that can have explosive consequences depending on the degree of separation of boys and girls and the degree to which traditional sex roles within the ethnic culture are dimorphic and separate.

Part of ethnic identity is a set of meanings assigned to various activities: to verbal discussion, for example, and to playing games, which may be perceived as appropriate activities only for children. The suggestion that a group sing a song may be viewed as delightful, artistic, and self-affirming, assuming that a worker or a member has not unwittingly selected a song that has a toxic political, social, or historical connotation for group members. Or, it may be viewed as a violation of adult (male, female, or both) dignity, a putdown, a source of embarrassment for group members who are not musically talented, and so on.

Unless a social worker is genuinely expert in understanding a particular culture, it is generally appropriate to ask before one tells, to let the group members be one's teachers about the use of nonverbal activities, in general, and the meaning of specific activities in particular. Sometimes activities that seem innocent enough have other meanings to group members. One of the authors once had the experience of suggesting a walk in a nearby park to a group of immigrants newly arrived in this country and this particular community. The idea went over like a lead balloon. Several meetings later one of the bolder group members shared with the worker, with considerable difficulty, the fact that in the Eastern European society from which the group members had emigrated, "a walk in the park" was a euphemism for being arrested by the secret police.

Ethnic patterns of respect and deference may differ markedly from those of the dominant American culture. In the eyes of most, if not all, social workers, American society is rife with inequalities of power and influence. In relation to many of the world's societies, however, contemporary American society is not only equalitarian, but sometimes amorphous to the point of seeming to be totally without rules or limits. Traditional patterns of deference, for example, or of who speaks first in a group, or who may be contradicted by whom, may be very important to group members of a particular ethnic group, or race, or culture. It is not part of the role of a social worker to tramp around like the proverbial bull in a china shop, ignoring and violating customs and ethnocultural patterns. It may well be part of a worker's role to help a group discuss, confront, and evaluate its own patterns or its ethnocultural pattern of behavior in groups. This needs to be based on awareness and information, as well as group readiness, not on ignorance and insensitivity.

One particular area in which there may be conflict between ethnic traditions and worker expectations pertains to patterns of sex roles and rules. What boys do and do not do, what girls do and do not do, and similar rules for adult men and women and for older people—these rules are often very important to people, regardless of their ethnic identities. We need not agree with these rules and patterns. Indeed, they may he at least mildly repugnant to some American social workers. This is not the point, however. Social workers in groups are on shaky ground indeed when *we* take on the roles of judging others' cultures, values, and relationship patterns.

There will, of course, be limits to a worker's own acceptance of cultural relativism, as there should be. Consider child abuse and domestic violence. Social workers have a moral, professional, ethical, and legal responsibility not to condone such behaviors. On the other hand, especially when dealing with fairly recent immigrants, whether from overseas or just from different communities, there may need to be an educational process in which the social worker takes part. Behaviors judged proper and normal in other cultures may be felonies in our own. The same perspective should be applied to child-rearing techniques, to ways of dealing with deviant behavior within an ethnic community, and, complicated though this may be, to the ingestion or other use of substances which are illegal or whose use is deviant in our society.

All ethnic groups distinguish between "us" and "them." Many, of course, distinguish various levels or types of them, and more than a few distinguish among various levels or types of us as well. Often, these latter distinctions are hidden from outsiders in the name of a sense of racial or ethnic solidarity; the distinctions are very well known to insiders, however.

The distinctions between "us" and "them" are not necessarily favorable to "us." As has been suggested here, self-hatred and self-deprecation may operate in such a way as to contrast the way "we" act with the way "they"—the dominant group(s), the powerful, the "real Americans"—behave. A homely but telling example has to do with the use of time. More than one minority group in American society has the idea that its members are not as punctual as "they." In fact, such a view is part of the folklore of some African Americans (for whom CPT [Colored People's Time] refers to a supposed lack of punctuality) and of Chinese Americans, especially on the West Coast (for whom CPT [Chinese People's Time] refers to the same phenomenon) and of Jews, whose self-deprecation about a lack of punctuality sometimes takes the form of a mild, but telling, ethnic joke. Needless to say, there is no scientific evidence to support any of these stereotypes, nor is it hard to find African Americans, Chinese Americans, or Jews who are meticulously prompt. The issue is a sense of one's own group not being quite up to snuff. In short, the issue is self-hatred, though of a mild, often humorous, and even occasionally warm and fuzzy kind.[1]

It is important for the social worker, of course, to recognize that there are things that one can say about oneself, about one's family, or, as the street saying goes, about one's sister which others cannot say. It is grossly insensitive, and potentially dangerous to an appropriate professional relationship, for a social worker not himself or herself part of an ethnic group to refer to "insider," self-deprecating remarks or jokes. Such insensitivities have been forced upon oppressed groups for many generations; they constitute a form of verbal racism, which really constitutes harassment, in the views of the authors.

Each person, in the course of growing up, is taught rules that govern various forms of social interaction with other persons. These rules may govern interactions with persons of the same age, younger, or older; powerful persons or persons viewed as less powerful than oneself; members of the same or opposite sex; and one of us or one of them. Ever since acute observers such as Goffman (1961) turned their attention to identifying these rules, their existence has seemed obvious. What may not be as obvious is the fact that these rules are not the same in different ethnocultural groups. Consider the issue of looking another person directly in the eyes. In some Latino cultures, and some others, looking an older person directly in the eyes is an act of marked disrespect.

[1]It is interesting to note that each minority group views itself as being chronically late, while it views the dominant group as being punctual.

Example

> An Anglo police officer confronts a Latino adolescent male. The latter looks down at the ground while the officer asks him a question. The police officer says, "Look at me when I talk to you!" The adolescent, certainly ill at ease to begin with, as most people are when being interrogated by a police officer, looks up. Then, realizing he is violating the customs of a lifetime, he looks down again. An angry altercation ensues. Each person feels violated by the other when, in effect, each is following a rule book for interaction. The two rule books are just different. The same rules that were taught to the Latino adolescent are also a part of some Asian American cultures. So are prohibitions against touching another person on the head, which is thought to constitute interference with the essence of someone's personality and spirituality.[2]

Another example is illustrated by Karnik and Suri (1995). They note that the people of India have a complex and unique system of religious and cultural beliefs and values that have profound influences on the social dynamics of Indian society. One historically predominant belief has been termed the *doctrine of karma or law of karma*. The law of karma can be defined as a fundamental Indian (Hindu) social value which states that an individual's total human condition is the summation of all past actions. Thus, the law of karma provides a value-oriented explanation for an individual's life condition.

India is, of course, a country of many ethnic groups; although Karnik and Suri conflate Indian and Hindu beliefs, clearly they are not entirely congruent. Also, Indian Americans differ as to the extent to which the ways of the "old country" and its beliefs persevere and persist in their encounters in American society. In general, however, an Indian American for whom the law of karma explains at least a major part of an individual's current condition is likely to view what happens in a small group, as well as in the larger society, through a very different lens than other members of this society.

The composition of a group is extremely important. The proportions of members of various identities, of degrees of homogeneity and heterogeneity, of single-sex or both sexes and the age span represented by the membership, the unique position of "onlys" and the stresses and misperceptions to which they are liable—all of these and others have been iden-

[2]We are indebted to Joan C. Weiss for this example.

tified as important for group process and for the experience that members are likely to have.

We are concerned here with ethnic identities and with the perceptual and affective lenses with which they equip members of their groups. These lenses enable those who have them to see, experience, and understand certain things very clearly and others not so clearly, to make certain attributions and not other attributions, to consider some behaviors normative and others deviant, and to actualize certain rules and patterns for interactions and not others. In groups, however, there are several possibilities that complicate the picture still further.

When the worker and the group members are of the same ethnocultural identity, this may make for ready acceptance by each of the other. It may also cause its own complexities. Group members may value or devalue the worker's ethnic identity when it is the same as theirs. There is the danger of a negative judgment of the worker, who is not a "real ___." In the current atmosphere, in which self-hatred is at least officially frowned upon, such a perception is less likely than it once was.

All group members may be of a particular ethnocultural identity, with the worker being different. As Proctor and Davis note (1994), for many minority groups in American society, it is likely that a considerable volume of social services will be provided to them by social workers who are not of their own ethnicity or racial identity. This makes it important for social workers, including those who work with groups, to be educated and aware of the potentials both for misunderstandings and conflict and for bridging gaps that exist in this situation. The membership of the group may be mixed racially, ethnically, and culturally. The worker may share an ethnic identity with one part of the group, or may be of a different ethnicity from any of those represented in the group. In some ways this is a potentially creative mix; in others, it maximizes the potential difficulties of effective communication, the establishment of intimacy and trust, and the development of a sense of safety in the group for both members and worker.

The group may have been formed around a shared characteristic, condition, challenge, or transition point. The members may all be people who have recently been widowed, say, or who have children diagnosed with cancer, who have been victims of abuse, or who are recovering from serious head injuries. While the members' (and worker's) ethnic identities are part of the group's collective identity, as they always are, they are less salient and affect the group's interactive processes less because, in such instances, the difference is less of a difference because it makes less of a difference. In such groups, as in many others, what unites the members is more important to them than their differences. Often, such groups are suffused with a sense of the common human condition that the members share, while ethnic differences that might have been enormously influential under other circumstances are virtually forgotten. In such groups, members often comment about how insignificant the differences among them seem.

Some Practice Principles, Briefly Stated

There is no lack, fortunately, of well-designed and thoughtful texts on group work (e.g., Brown, 1991; Garvin, 1996; Gitterman and Shulman, 1994; Glassman and Kates, 1990; Greif and Ephross, 1997; Henry, 1992; Northen, 1988; Toseland and Rivas, 1995). Virtually all contain lists of practice principles, as well as case illustrations of a wide variety of types of groups. All state principles of social justice, equality, and social goals. All teach methods and skills that are applicable to working with groups composed of ethnically identified people. We shall, therefore, confine ourselves here to mentioning briefly a few practice principles that are particularly brought to the fore by the discussion in this chapter, and leave the integration of general practice principles to the reader.

No worker can be expert on all cultures. Many of us, indeed, spend our careers trying, not necessarily successfully, to understand our own culture in depth, and perhaps to become acquainted with one other. But there is no need to try to be an all-culture expert. Let your group members be your teachers. This will yield positive results both for them and for you.

- Try to observe Redl's Law of Optimum Distance (1953), which states that one should try to avoid having one of anything in a group. Being the only anything makes one vulnerable to feeling lonely in the midst of a group and also increases the probability that one will be either scapegoated or treated like a mascot.
- Discuss with members of the group, preferably with the entire group, the goals, purposes, and procedures of the group. Expect a period of testing on the part of the group. Members of various ethnic groups have suffered exceedingly, either at the hands of people who look like you or at the hands of others in their countries of origin, during the immigration experience or since arriving. Do not be surprised that the group does not immediately understand your role as a worker in a benign and trusting way or their roles as group members.
- Allow time for discussion, questions, introductions, and consideration of issues. In many ethnic cultures—sometimes, indeed, in American soci-

ety as a whole, though this is often not admitted—time equals love and caring. Being fobbed off with a quick remark and a glance at the power person's watch conveys a message of disrespect and is often experienced as a rejection.

- It is almost inevitable that sooner or later in a group's life some members' feelings will be hurt, some will feel misunderstood, and some will be offended by what is done or said by other members of the group. This does not reflect badly on the worker (or on the group). Such hurt, misunderstanding, and other feelings are part of the reality of the group, part of its life space, and are good topics with which the group can deal.

  As a worker, adopt a position of cultural relativism and the stance of a learner, to the extent that you can without violating meaningful values or perceptions of your own. When matters come up in the group from which you feel an ethical need to dissent, do so, provided that you have thought about it for at least a few seconds, preferably longer.

- Naiveté ill becomes a professional social worker. Neither shock nor losing control should be part of a professional's stock of role behaviors.
- Your investment in the group needs to be in the group-as-a-whole. The group is not merely a setting for the "treatment" of individuals. Avoid siding with one part of a group or the other; side with the group-as-a-whole.

  Group treatment should be the treatment of choice for many members of many ethnocultural groups. The reason is that groups are safer for members. They can get support from each other. Members can interpret, both in the direct, linguistic dimension, and in the less direct, nonverbal dimension. Group work is not ancillary to the "real" work which takes place with individuals. In fact, very often groups should be the primary loci of help, support, treatment, and learning.

  Help the group develop their own instruments and forms such as questionnaires and parties, to assess and celebrate its own accomplishments. One thinks of involving family members when children's groups are being assessed but rarely thinks of adult groups in the same way. Perhaps it is time for such involvements.

- While being sharply aware of the importance of ethnic identities in groups, avoid stereotyping. Not all ______s are alike. Ethnic identity serves as a guideline, not as a prescription.
- Celebrate diversity and help the groups you work with do the same. Diversity enriches group life; differences are to be welcomed and explored, not feared and kept hidden.

Working Through the Ethnic Lens

Throughout this book, we utilize the metaphor of lenses, ground and polished by socialization within both an ethnic community and the broader American society, and focused by the individual experiences of the client and the worker. In groups, the situation is a bit more complicated, which is one of the characteristics that gives groups their unique power to affect both individuals and society. We are referring here to the fact that the group-as-a-whole, as it forms, develops what is, in effect, its own lens or system of lenses, both ethnic and unique to the particular group.

The same cautions and guidelines apply in groups as with other kinds of client systems. It is important for a social worker in a group to keep a broad field of vision, one which allows the worker to encompass the individual group members, the group as a whole, the sponsoring organization, and the broader societal backdrop against which group life takes place. Which one will take priority in demanding the worker's attention and participation will vary from group to group and from phase to phase within a particular group's life. But the reader will not be surprised to learn that, in our view, the pattern of attention and interaction within a group will, in general, also contain reflections of the ethnic identities of members, worker, and sponsoring organization.

A Case Vignette for Study

The group, who quickly named themselves the "Thrivers" at their first meeting, after having rejected the suggestion of "Survivors," was made up of 9 or 10 (one was uncertain about his interest) 12- to 14-year-old boys. All lived in public housing, all had been victims, either intended or incidental, of physical assaults or confrontations within the past year or so. All had been referred to the group by school personnel for help with dealing with the effects of having been assaulted, and all knew each other.

Questions for Discussion

1. If you were the worker with the Thrivers, how would you have prepared for the first meeting, in light of the contents of this chapter?

2. Assume that you are African American and male. How would this have affected your preparation? How may it affect your behavior as group worker?
3. Assume that you are African American and female. How would this have affected your preparation? How may it affect your behavior as group worker?
4. One of the basic responsibilities of a social worker in a group is helping the group set limits for its members' behavior. Is this affected by the ethnic identity of the members? Similarly at different ages? Differently at different ages?
5. Should one plan a group's time frame (short-term, long-term, and decided by whom) differently depending on the ethnic identity of the members? Why, or why not?

References

Bertcher, H. J. (1994). *Group Participation: Techniques for Leaders and Members* (2nd ed.). Thousand Oaks, CA: Sage.

Brown, L. N. (1991). *Groups for Growth and Change*. New York: Longman.

Ephross, P. H. (1997). Introduction. In G. L. Greif and P. H. Ephross (Eds.), *Group Work with Populations at Risk*. New York: Oxford University Press.

Ephross, P. H., and Vassil, T. V. (1988). *Groups that Work: Structure and Process*. New York: Columbia University Press.

Falck, H. S. (1988). *Social work: The Membership Perspective*. New York: Springer.

Garvin, C. D. (1987). *Contemporary Group Work* (2nd ed.). Englewood Cliffs, NJ: Prentice Hall.

Garvin, C. D. (1996). *Contemporary Group Work* (3rd ed.). Boston: Allyn and Bacon.

Gitterman, A., and Shulman, L. (Eds.). (1994). *Mutual Aid Groups, Vulnerable Populations and the Life Cycle* (2nd ed.). New York: Columbia University Press.

Glassman, U., and Kates, L. (1990). *Group Work: A Humanistic Approach*. Newbury Park, CA: Sage.

Goffman, E. (1961). *Asylums: Notes on the Social Situation of Mental Patients and Other Inmates*. Garden City, NY: Doubleday.

Greif, G. L., and Ephross, P. H. (Eds.). (1997). *Group Work with Populations at Risk*. New York: Oxford University Press.

Henry, S. (1992). *Group Skills in Social Work* (2nd ed.). Itasca, IL: F. E. Peacock.

Karnik, S. J., and Suri, K. B. (1995). The law of karma and social work considerations. *International Social Work, 38*, 365–377.

Middleman, R. R. (1988). *The Non-Verbal Method in Social Work with Groups* (expanded ed.). Hebron, CT: Practitioners Press.

Northen, H. (1988). *Social Work with Groups* (2nd ed.). New York: Columbia University Press.

Proctor, E. K., and Davis, L. E. (1994). The challenge of racial difference: Skills for clinical practice, *Social Work, 39*, 314–373.

Redl, F. (1953). The art of group composition. In S. Schulze (Ed.), *Creative Group Living in a Children's Institution.* (pp. 76–96). New York: Association Press.

Toseland, R. W., and Rivas, R. (1995). *An Introduction to Group Work Practice* (2nd ed.). New York: Macmillan.

4

Ethnicity and Families

> Our sense of uniqueness, of being rooted in one space to one group, comes from our membership in families. It is through the experiences of growing up within the confines of the family that we first begin to get a sense of who we are, what we are, and what direction our lives will take. When we examine ourselves, we find that who we are and who we can become depend in great part upon who we started out to be. This is found within our families. Our ethnicity cannot be separated from our families. Within the security and insecurity of our families, as they face all of the developmental changes that families must, by definition, go through, we become firmly established in our time and place. . . . What do we mean by *family ethnicity?* . . . An individual's family ethnicity clearly establishes the core of his or her being. . . . *Family ethnicity* has come to mean the interaction of all elements that occur within ethnic family constellations.
>
> H. P. McAdoo, *Family Ethnicity: Strength in Diversity*

These are soaring statements, optimistic at a time in which it is fashionable to view families as dysfunctional, as settings for the expression of psychopathologies and the practice of abuse, or as places in which lessons are taught which have to be unlearned, sometimes painfully, later in life. In fact, when it comes to families, we believe that McAdoo is correct on balance. Ethnic parents and community leaders know this and place great emphasis on what goes on within the family, for they know that continuity and health both depend on the strength of families.

One needs to take account of two cautions. For some, their early experiences in families, or in foster or institutional care, which took its place, have indeed been painful and destructive. For a blessed few, early family experiences were entirely wonderful. For most of humanity, however, families have expressed both their strengths and their weaknesses as they have transmitted their cultures, especially ethnic cultures, and provided the conditions for their children to acquire all that McAdoo lists. Our experiences in families are the most important and influential of our lives.

When one wants to signify closeness, solidarity, and mutual supportiveness, be it at work (legal or otherwise), on the sports field, while climbing mountains, or just with friends, Americans say, "We're like a family!" Even when the family's reality does not reach the ideal, the concept of family is a sort of icon or prototype of a caring and cohesive group. In groups, members often express a sense of closeness, support, and being valued by drawing an analogy between the other group members and their families. One often hears statements like, "To me, you are family," or "my brothers and sisters," while analogies are often drawn between the group worker and a parent or older sibling. For half a century we have had the benefit of the studies which are collectively identified with *The Authoritarian Personality* (Adorno, Frenkel-Brunswick, Levinson, and Sanford, 1950), and have known scientifically what others thought for millennia. That is, our picture of the Deity, often called "Heavenly Father" or, to be up-to-date, "Sovereign and Parent," is related to our picture of our earthly father or parent.

Families transmit cultures. Ethnic families within American society transmit the cultures that define both the family and the people who are its members. Families teach languages, dialects, and particular adaptations of languages. Even more important, families are dictionaries and encyclopedias; they teach the meaning of words, the history of concepts, and their definitions.

They are powerful agencies through which cultures socialize their members' emotions. In a sense, then, families teach you what and how you speak and what and how you feel, when, and to what extent. Experiences in families—and, for some in our society, in collectivities that serve as surrogates for families—teach what is normative and what is deviant for a great many aspects of life. A partial listing of these aspects begins the next section of this chapter.

Most important for the purposes of this book, *families define ethnicity*. They teach about the homeland and the history of the ethnic group both in the homeland and here. They define who are us and who are they, thus teaching the boundaries of the ethnic group and acquainting a child with both ethnic history and a series of meanings to attribute to it. The ethnic lens, which plays a central part in the model of ethnicity adopted in this book, is formulated, ground, polished, and fitted in one's family. Children, often at a surprisingly early age, learn who "we" are, how we both do and are supposed to act, what "they" think of us and how they treat us, what parts of what they do and say to take seriously and what to overlook.

If the reader is even a bit skeptical on this point, an experiment is in order. Tomorrow, or tonight, or perhaps when you have finished a reading assignment in this book, select a couple of hours at random. During that time, listen to your mother's or your father's voice or both inside your own head. (If you weren't raised by one or both parents, listen to the voices of the people who did raise you.) Comment on everything that happens (silently, if you want, so others don't think you strange) as your parent would were she or he there in person. Focus, for the purpose of this experiment, on ethnic-relevant matters such as food, family matters, daily events in your community, and perceptions of "us" and "them." Note how easy this is. Pay attention to how many of your parents' perceptions, attitudes, and emotions you can easily re-create, because they are a part of you. Notice how well you have integrated the lens that guided perception and the feelings about self and others stimulated by those perceptions. Note the norms, implicit and explicit, that inform your statements. Were you aware that you carried so many of your parents' definitions and ethnic characteristics in yourself?

Gender and Ethnicity

Gender and ethnicity are linked in several ways. Referring to white ethnics, Alba (1990) notes:

> Women view their ethnic backgrounds as more important than men do by a considerable margin. Among ethnic identifiers with single ancestry, women were twice as likely as men to rate their ethnic backgrounds as very important. . . . One possible explanation lies in the close linkage between ethnicity and family in the minds of many respondents. Since women typically are charged with greater responsibility for maintaining family relationships and traditions . . . they tend to see ethnicity, at least in the specific sense of family origins, as quite important. (pp. 69–70)

For various immigrant groups, leaving home and coming to the United States involved a change in the status of many women from homemakers, parents, and participants in multigenerational family processes to members of the labor force. Changes in sex role definitions within families often accompany this change. Studies of two different kinds of ethnic families focus on the changes in women's roles, both inside and outside the family, and the resultant changes in the structure and content of female-male relationships within families. The first refers to Latin American families and clearly relates women's work roles to changes in the direction of more egalitarianism in general, perhaps with particular reference to sexual morality.

> The double standard of sexual morality, along with the concept of male dominance, has prevailed in Cuban culture. . . . However, as shown above concerning Mexican and Puerto Rican families in the United States, when women work outside the home, egalitarian values and behaviors tend to emerge. (Chilman, 1993, p. 156)

The second, part of a description of the Muslim family in North America, demonstrates clearly not only the influence of women's work outside the home on patterns of male-female relationships within the family, but also the effects of intergenerational processes of assimilation on the experiences of young women and, in turn, the effects of these experiences on ethnoreligious traditional definitions of appropriate behavior for Islamic daughters. Note, especially, the value placed on endogamous (within the ethnic group) marriage, a value which often has less salience for the native-born generation than for their immigrant parents. We cite the next writer at some length because he enlightens us on the relationships among variables which might otherwise be thought quite separate.

> Perhaps the most significant impact [of immigrating to the United States] was on the lives of Muslim women. The overall expectation of the traditional role of the Muslim woman is not very different from that of many other ethnic and religious groups: as a mother, she is the anchor of the family; as a wife, her role is to complement and enhance the image of her husband; and as a homemaker, she is the one on whom the bulk of responsibility falls for the organization and maintenance of the household. These traditional role expectations still constitute a norm in most Muslim families, but clearly some fundamental changes have taken place in the lives of Muslim women in America. The most important is the transition of women from the sphere of work in the private space within the house to the realm of public space in the American workplace. This has meant that the essentially separate worlds of Muslim men and women in the public spheres have now become fused. . . .
>
> The stresses that mark intergenerational conflict are as much in evidence among Muslims as among other tradition-oriented American groups. Some of these are seen as superficial pandering to aspects of American youth behavior, such as dating, drinking, and so forth, particularly as far as girls are concerned. Coupled with this is the fear of intermarriage. Again, Muslim girls, who, according to traditional Islamic law, are forbidden to marry outside the faith, represent a vulnerable area of stress in Muslim families. In general, as the new generation grows up, the intergenerational gap in per-

> ception of North American versus the past home-country system of values tends to grow wider. (Nanji, 1993, pp. 236–237)

There are wide variations, of course, among ethnic groups. In general, though, it seems fair to say that the largely traditional cultural patterns of many groups include a strongly dimorphic view of what is appropriate for men and for women, a rather strict division of labor within the family, a patriarchal structure of power and authority within the family, and stringent controls on the expression of women's sexuality. These patterns are under attack from the patterns of the dominant American culture, whose trends seem in each instance to threaten to overwhelm the most deeply felt norms and expectations of the tradition-oriented Muslim community in America.

Family Ethnicity: Some Variables

We began with an attempt to list the important variables of family life which are affected by ethnicity and which may come to be the foci of attention for a social worker working with a family. To our surprise, when we had finished listing just the areas which we thought were of priority importance, there were 18. For every area, we were able to list several questions, each of which represented a specific variable under the general heading. It seemed clearly impractical to discuss each specific variable with regard to interventions or influence technologies. What we shall do is to list the 18 headings, together with the specific variables related to each. We shall comment, at least briefly, on the issues for social work practice and for the practitioner raised by each.

A few cautions should be pointed out first. We do not think that what follows is a complete list, by any means. Nor will all of these be foci of attention for any given family nor for all families within a particular ethnic group. Each, however, may be part of the reason why a family has come for help, whether that family has come *en groupe* for family therapy, or whether a particular family member is the identified client.

Specific Variable	*Aspect of Life*
Language(s)	Which one to speak? If more than one, where and when is each to be spoken? With whom?

What is most significant about languages is that there is a cognitive structure built into the ways that concepts are expressed. There are also connotations associated with speaking a particular language. For example, a Latina who speaks Spanish with her grandmother will associate some of her feelings for her grandmother with the language. A family that raises a bilingual child is giving that child a priceless gift, in our opinion, precisely because bilingualism implies biculturalism, the ability to function in two cultures. Social workers, who have always needed to be multilingual in a symbolic sense, need to pay much more attention to becoming bi- or multilingual in a literal sense. Being able to communicate with hearing-impaired people through sign language makes this point clear. (For the purposes of this discussion, we may consider the hearing impaired to constitute an "ethnic group.")

Speech norms	Who speaks first? Last? When? Are there forbidden subjects? What about talking at mealtimes? What about curse words and other obscenities?

Related to these issues is the question that pops up throughout this book of who is "entitled" to speak for the family. This is important for social work practice because the spokesperson is often also the one entitled to ask for help for a family member. Also, many ethnic families have strongly held norms about who can talk about what, particularly to an outsider like a social worker. We should not overlook or regard these norms lightly.

Religion and religious practices	Which one? How seriously? Are there rituals practiced at home? "Does God live with the family?" Is there conflict about religion? Ambivalence? What is the content of the religion?

As this book is being written, some see a reawakening of interest in and respect for religious principles and behaviors within social work. This trend may make it easier for social workers in the future to recognize the power and importance that religion and religious practices have for many ethnic families (as well as others.) The writers of this book are simultaneously committed to two points of view. The one sets boundaries and forbids proselytizing on the part of social workers. The second points to the central importance of recognizing the part that religion, whichever it is specifically, plays in the lives of families.

Sex role behaviors	What do boys do? Girls? Women? Men? What constitutes success for females? Males? Are these criteria of success the same or different? Who makes decisions within the family? Why? (Is there an informal as well as a formal structure.) What life course is visualized for women and men, boys and girls? Are there strains between traditional ethnic expectations and trends within American society regarding sex role definitions?

We have touched on some of the ways in which different sex role behavioral expectations may cause strains within traditional Muslim families, but they are by no means the only ones experiencing such strains. Many ethnic families and communities find themselves in the midst of multiple forces and currents of change both within their own ethnic community and within the broader American society. Changing expectations of boys and girls, women and men affect work, child care, standards of dress, educational patterns, behaviors within the family and in the broader community, patterns of child care and child-rearing, and many other areas of family life. At the same time, many of these areas are undergoing change within American families and within the dominant cultural frame.

Sex education and behavioral standards	"Does sex live in the house?" Is it ever talked about? Verbally and nonverbally, what are the "messages," whether transmitted directly or indirectly, by omission or by implication?

There are few topics that raise as strong feelings as does sex. Yet sexual issues, behaviors, yearnings, and problems are intricately interwoven with a surprisingly large proportion of clinical social work practice. Sexuality also interacts with issues of relatedness and loneliness, intimacy and isolation, and many others that are of concern to clients and to workers. Sexual issues have intertwined with racism and prejudice; this is one of the reasons why communication about sexuality across ethnic boundaries is very difficult.

We wish to stress a few points for practitioners, recognizing that we are dealing with a topic which, in our view, needs much more attention than it has received in the social work curricula and the social work literature. *First*, be alert to the possibility of sexual issues underlying presenting problems. *Second*, be careful because of the sensitivity of the subject. If you are going to bring up sexual issues, explain why you are doing so and be sure that the words you use are clearly understood. Alternatively, ask the client what words he or she uses for various feelings, acts, and problems.

Do not communicate across gender boundaries about sex unless and until you have enough knowledge and comfort with the culture to know what you are doing. The possibilities for misunderstanding, feelings of discomfort, and boundary violation are greatest in this situation for heterosexual people.

For the same reason, do not make jokes about sexual subjects. Firm believers in the communicative and therapeutic potential of humor as both authors are, this is not the subject about which to make jokes. They are too easily misunderstood.

Be aware of and alert to the meanings of physical touch. Touch carries powerful meanings in some ethnic cultures, both for good and for threat. It is important to know what you are communicating before you touch adolescents or adults. Children are, in general, safer to touch, especially when parents or relatives are present.

Finally, at the risk of offending the reader, we are moved to remind you of the importance of maintaining proper professional boundaries, including, but not limited to, sexual behavior. Sexual behavior between social worker and client is always destructive to the client and fraught with danger for the worker. It is a violation of professional ethics in all of the helping professions, specifically including social work.

Education of children	How important? What kind? What content? To what end? What is a good reason for absence? How are grades viewed? What about child rearing in general?

Ethnoracial cultures vary greatly in their views of proper child rearing, in their expectations of children at particular ages and stages, and in their views of proper relationships between children and adults. At the same time, virtually all ethnic groups invest a great deal of pride and take an enormous interest in *their* children.

Money	Importance? How obtained? How treated? Symbolic meanings? How spent? Investments? By whom? In what? How decided?

Family identity and obligation	Responsibility for relatives? Aging parents? Sib lings? Time to be spent? Involvement of relatives in decision making?

Sometimes without intention, social workers are perceived as being on the "self-fulfillment" side of what has become a major issue of controversy in American society, rather than on what some political figures like to call the "family values" side. This is a strange and unrealistic characterization of social work, for our concern with families dates from the earliest years of the profession. Respect for differences is easy in the abstract. For some social work practitioners, respecting attitudes very different from one's own is much more difficult.

Interethnic relations	How are other ethnic groups viewed? Is there a hierarchy? Are any "like us"?

In much of the world, ethno-racial-cultural identity is taken very seriously indeed. However much we discuss diversity, most social workers are uncomfortable with the custom of attributing abilities, philosophies, and personal characteristics on the basis of ethnic identity. This practice is, in fact, often identified as racist. Whether or not one thinks along these lines, members of many groups attribute certain characteristics to "us" and to "them," and "they" are rarely thought of as monolithic. Working with members of diverse ethnic groups does not require us to change our own perceptions, but rather to hear others' with some equanimity and regard.

The annual calendar	Which holidays and occasions are observed? How? Where? Who is included? What's eaten or not eaten? Drunk or not drunk?

A good way to prepare one's consciousness for working with others who observe different customs is to review one's own customs.

The life cycle: stages and phases	What are the stages of life? What are the signs of passage from one to another? How old does one need to be to do ____? Does one defer to the elderly? To what extent? On what kinds of issues?

No group separates the life cycle from biological realities. There is a good deal of freedom, though, within biologically set limits, for social construction of the life cycle. For example, the stage of adolescence, especially in its extended form now seen throughout American culture in the broad sense, is relatively unknown among many ethnic groups, for whom there is a relatively quick transition from child to adult. Many family issues revolve around these different and sometimes conflictual definitions of the life cycle. Acculturation sounds like a rather bloodless concept until one talks with an ethnic adolescent who wants to be an American teenager but whose parents simply do not "connect" with the concept.

Time: the pattern of a day, a week, a year	What time does and should one get up in the morning? Go to sleep at night? Eat meals? Brush one's teeth? Do one's homework?

The whole issue of time impinges most directly on social work practitioners in the form of appointments for interviews and meetings. Members of the dominant, middle-class, American culture, as are social workers and other human service professionals, live lives that revolve around clocks, times, and appointments. Such a way of organizing life is quite alien to many ethnic persons and families.

Work, jobs, career	Who works? At what? How hard? For whom? What happens to whose paycheck? Do children work? At what age(s)? What happens to family members' earnings? Is the family cashbox visualized as communal and collective, in the sense that everyone's earnings go into it and everyone's needs are taken care of by it? Or do children, wives, husbands have money that is or should be their "own"?
Alcohol and other drugs	Forbidden? Allowed? To whom? At what age? In what context?

This variable and its potential for interaction with other issues would seem to be obvious. Convinced as many Americans are that problems around ingested substances are worst in our society, we forget the universality of some forms of drug-taking behavior.

Criminal behavior, arrest, incarceration, and so on	How viewed? How and treated? Reactions to these events by others? By Family members? How does the family handle issues of shame, guilt, fault and the practical matters of getting a lawyer, meeting the needs of family members who are incarcerated, and so on?

Social workers who work in correctional systems (whether juvenile or adult), or with court services related to punishment and incarceration, or in probation or parole services need not only understanding but also highly developed communication skills. Various ethnic lenses perceive the experience of family members, the nature of the correctional system, and how to relate to personnel, including social workers, within it, very differently. One should not be surprised, given a long history of racism and unequal treatment of suspected and convicted offenders. Historically, it is fair to say that poor people and members of racial and ethnic minorities have borne the brunt of severity and inhumanity, and their families the brunt of both poverty and stigma. Somewhat defensively, "doing time" has become a badge of honor in some communities, especially among young men in metropolitan inner cities.

Illness and medical treatment; counseling, ness? advice, and help	General perceptions? Whom to go to for diagnosis and treatment of physical ill- Mental illness? What are acceptable treatments? Whom to turn to for advice and help?

There is abundant evidence from the field of medical sociology about differential ethnic behavior and experiential patterns around pain, illness, treatment, disfigurement, family caretaking, and dealing with death. This subject is discussed in greater detail in chapter 7.

Charity	Given to whom? How much? Who decides?

Most "outsiders" are unaware of the extent to which ethnic charities and service organizations, which range from informal and family-based to complex and formal, enable ethnic community members to survive, gain educations, and start businesses and careers. They also supplement family care of elderly and infirm members of the community and alleviate the effects of disasters such as floods, fires, and hurricanes. Sometimes, as in the case of the Jewish community, the organizations are community-wide. In other instances, a particular church or religious grouping within an ethnic community is the sponsor of a program.

Several ethnic charities have developed over the generations by providing life and disability and other forms of insurance, often at lower cost than elsewhere and always in the native language of immigrants or within the communities and cultural patterns of ethnoracial groups. Ethnic building and loan societies are major sources of mortgage money for home buyers and owners in many urban and suburban communities. African-American sororal and fraternal organizations have involved themselves in finding adoption homes, providing scholarships for needy students, and lobbying for adequate social welfare provision.

Social workers, especially those who do not identify with ethnic communities, have sometimes been signally unaware of these potential sources of help for clients, as well as the potential such organizations offer for community reintegration.

Intimate partner relationships	Expectations? Patterns of behavior, sexual and otherwise? Who defers to whom? Power balance? Spheres of influence?

This is a crucial area for both assessment and treatment, not only for family treatment but also for any attempt to modify couple relationships and relieve distress. Ethnic communities' emphases on families include stress on marriage and, in the case of some, on other committed relationship forms. One writer has noted,

> [in the African American community] a family's survival depends on spousal cooperation in the gathering of scarce resources in order to be able to exchange them with others in their society. The perceived power of the family unit may be seen as depending on the unit's ability to survive and defend itself. (J. L. McAdoo, 1993, p. 110)

As McAdoo points out, historically the ability of both partners to work together for the family's common good has been not just a matter of preference but also of necessity for the family's and the community's survival.

There are several inferences to be drawn which are relevant for practice. As can be seen, there are a great many variables within any given family. Ethnic patterns influence virtually all of the aspects just listed and many of the variables that are embedded within each. Some examples may help to illustrate this point. One of the areas of potential conflict and, sometimes, great pain in a family is the contrast between the "old country" or "down home" patterns and those which characterize the American ethnic group. This pattern affects many Asian-American families. A Korean-American woman may have very different life cycle, economic, and career expectations, as well as different expectations of the relationship between husband and wife, than a woman from Korea.

The old idea that America is a "melting pot" that melts ethnic differences is clearly not true. On the other hand, if it does not melt, it does rather soften some rough edges. Perhaps one could say that entry into American society shapes patterns of difference but does not melt them. Italian-American families, like African-American (from Africa) families, have some similarities to, but also are different from, Italian families in Italy, as are African-American families from those in their African country of origin.

Another example concerns patterns of child rearing. Throughout much of the world, and for many ethnocultural groups in this society, child rearing is a focused, sometimes (in the view of the dominant American culture, biased as are all cultures' views) brutal process of parents working hard to recreate themselves in their children. One should also note that, since the dawn of recorded history, parents have bemoaned their inability precisely to 'clone' themselves in their children. The war between the generations is a very old one indeed, in most, if not all, cultures and countries.

Consider, then, the experience of, say, an African-American parent upon being told authoritatively that physical discipline constitutes child abuse. What may be invalidated is not only the parent, but also a multigenerational ethnic tradition which gives parents authority over their children, both for better and for worse. A challenge by a powerful, self-assured social worker to the personal adequacy, deep motivation, and parenting skills and methods of a parent, and the resultant blend of hostility and sense of inadequacy, may in our view do more harm to the child, and the child-parent relationship, than the means of discipline.

This brief example brings up some of the realities of life for ethnic parents, especially for first-generation immigrants. Often, the expressed motivation for exposing one's self and one's family to the strain and trauma of immigration is the desire to make a better life for one's children. Even with good community support and extended family help, which not all immigrants can count on, much of one's self-confidence can be lost in the process of beginning acculturation. Not knowing English well puts adults, especially parents, in the position of feeling inadequate and vulnerable, as well as obviously "different." Family power relationships, very important in the country of origin, often get stood on their head, both between husband and wife and between parents and children, as children often learn both the English language and American mores faster and more easily than their parents do.

Thus roles can become inverted, with the children or adolescents serving as authorities for their parents, explaining American ways, writing letters, or filling out forms for their parents, for example. Tension arises from the children's impatience with their parents and their ways, which are so unlike what they see on television and what they experience with the families of their nonimmigrant friends. Parents and grandparents may sense that they are sources of shame rather than respect on the part of their children. A sense of "losing one's children" to American ways, to unacceptable behavioral patterns, to indecent clothes and disrespectful behavior, can be as painful for parents as being on the receiving end of racism, nativism, and discrimination.

Many ethnic groups have long traditions of surviving under less-than-ideal, and in some cases brutal and oppressive, treatment by the majority society and the dominant culture. To tell the carriers of such traditions that their customs are wrong, their foods unhealthy, their patterns of community and family support ineffective, their patterns of intimate relationships dysfunctional and, perhaps most of all, that they are doing wrong and are inadequate as parents constitutes an assault against their own and their family's dignity and sense of worth. Leaving adults in the ethnic community ignorant of the standards, practices, and judgments of the broader society is not doing them a favor either. How can social workers serve as carriers of useful information and perspectives while supporting, rather than reducing, the sense of adequacy of adults and children alike?

Social Work Practice with Ethnic Families

The experience of ethnic families with social workers, and vice versa, can best be described as a "mixed bag." On the one hand, one can find any number of ethnically identified families who honor and appreciate the help they have received from one or more social workers. Such writers as Wood and Middleman (1989) spell out practice models that are particularly useful for working with ethnic families. Wood and Middleman define a kind of role flexibility and a willingness to operate in whatever role is needed in order to be helpful to the family, which seems well tailored to the often multiple needs of ethnic families. On the other hand, the all-knowing, supremely poised, non-ethnically identifiable social worker who symbolically carries a copy of the agency's policies at all times is not hard to find either, even today.

It has been suggested that, all other things being equal, families with strong ethnic identities would prefer to get help from members of their own group. In the experience of the writers, this is true of some people but not of others. Virtually all ethnic clients, especially heads of families, seek competence first. Members of ethnically identified communities know very well that someone who looks, acts, and talks like them may be delightful and helpful, or may be using their origins in common to carry on a scam, to manipulate, or for other nefarious purposes that are not in the best interests of the family that needs help. The opposite is also well known: the nonmember of one's ethnic group whose pattern of identifications, genuine desire to be helpful, and respect for the strengths and abilities of client families looms much larger in clients' eyes than the color of their skin or the accent of their speech.

Family Structure

One of the authors once spent an entire summer working with public school teachers and principals to develop one of four parts of a curriculum for health education for students in Maryland's public schools. The attempt was successful: with some modifications, most parts of the curriculum are still in use. Two memories remain from that experience: how hot it gets in many public schools without air conditioning in the summer, and how difficult it is to define the concept *family*. The reader is invited to try. Sit down with a blank piece of paper in front of you and try to write a definition. Once you have done that, find exceptions to what you have written: collectivities of people who do not fit your definition but nonetheless are, or feel as though they are, a family. The point, of course, is that one way to define a family is by experience. A person's family is composed of those people whom one considers to be family. In past generations, and still in some places, families were enlarged by people called by names like "Uncle X" or "Aunt Y," who were old family friends sharing living quarters, or sometimes boarders paying rent. They became what anthropologists call "classificatory kin," people classified as relatives even though this was not supported by either genetic or legal relatedness.

It is foolish and counterproductive to argue with, say, a child as to what are the limits of the family. If a child describes an adult male as his uncle, and feels toward and relates to that person as Uncle, what is the point of arguing with the child? Some ethnic groups not only define relationships unknown in the broader community, but for historical or other reasons may let people into the family in informal ways. An example of the first is the east European term, often but not necessarily identified with Jews, of "landsman" or "lantzman." The first in German, and the second in Yiddish, both denote someone from the same area as the speaker, often someone who emigrated from the same town. Informally, the terms denote someone with whom one shares significant aspects of background experience.

Religious Factors in Ethnic Identities

The predominant American culture, and thus the modal American family, can be characterized as secular. Though families may nominally be members of churches, religion and religious identity have not been viewed as integral to daily family life, nor to resolving family problems and crises. Whether or not the characterization of the broader society is accurate, it fails to describe the role of religion in many (by no means all) ethnic families.

For many white ethnics, church is either an important ongoing part of life or a haven and source of help in times of personal or family crisis. The same may be said of many fundamentalist Christian groups who, while not necessarily defined by their ethnicity, often function as ethnic groups in that they provide their members with the kind of lens that is comparable to the shared lens of an ethnic group. Religion has given hope and assuaged some of the worst effects of oppression for African Americans throughout their history. The viability, strength, and vitality of African-American churches are largely invisible to most whites.

This fact gives eloquent testimony to the extent to which segregation and the resulting ignorance are characteristics of contemporary urban life for most Americans. The reader is urged to become more familiar with what takes place at, say, 11:00 a.m. on Sunday mornings. Better still, visit an African-American church. If you are white and identified as a first-time guest, you may be pleased and moved by the warmth with which you are welcomed. One should also note the growth of two religious communities: the separatist black Muslims and the much less well publicized (Orthodox)

Muslim community among African Americans. Both are signs of a continued search for religious identity and a desire to integrate religion with other aspects of family life.

In many Latino communities, the parish priest is a part of the community who shares joys, tragedies, and community as well as family occasions. The growth and proliferation of Korean Protestant churches is one visible sign of the growth of this community, as is the development and growth in various cities of Buddhist, Hindu, and Islamic places of worship, schools, and community centers. A renewed interest in tribal religious practice has been noted among many American Indian nations. Religion, culture, history, and ethnicity are intertwined in the Jewish community, so that it is certainly possible to be Jewish and atheist—a fact that points to one of the core differences between Judaism and Christianity.

A recent revival of interest in the religious roots of social work and in religious and spiritual aspects of social work treatment and services has been well documented (DiBlasio, 1993; Enright and the Human Development Study Group, 1991; Worthington, 1993). There are also many social workers employed in sectarian agencies that are sponsored by one of several religious communities. For the most part, however, it is fair to say that a majority of professional social workers share the secularism of the broader society. This lack of fit between social workers and ethnic family clients may be another barrier to be bridged. If social workers' lenses and client families' lenses perceive different images, so to speak, when it comes to religious aspects of family life, it can be just that much harder to form an alliance for change, problem solving, or effective social action.

Life Cycle Issues and Ethnicity

The lens through which a person is socialized to view the life cycle, indeed to view life itself, is largely produced by ethnic identity, as we have repeatedly pointed out. It may be useful, before turning to some specifics of social work practice with ethnic families, to highlight certain points and processes in the life cycle that are particularly affected by ethnic identity and that, in turn, affect how one is viewed within an ethnically identified community. These are courtship and family formation, childbearing and child rearing, marriage and alternative relationship forms, the processes of aging, and the relationships between aged persons and their families. Emphasizing these aspects of the life cycle does not mean that they are the only important ones. Rather, they are both important and likely to be involved in transactions with social workers and social agencies, to loom large through the ethnic lenses of clients and applicants, and understanding them is crucial for social workers of all specializations and fields.

Each ethnic group is concerned with its own survival to an extent that ranges from considerable to overwhelming. The keys to demographic survival, of course, are courtship and marriage patterns, and childbearing and child rearing. The issues, aspirations, and realities of in-marriage and out-marriage, endogamy and exogamy, are often major issues, especially for the relationships between older adolescent and younger adult children and their middle-aged or aging parents. One factor in the tension is loyalty to the ethnic group and the desire of (potential) grandparents for grandchildren who are identified with the ethnocultural tradition that is important to them. Personal freedom and a view of love, commitment, and family formation provide the opposite pole. The outcome is mixed, with out-marriage certainly on the increase, especially in recent years (Alba, 1990; Glick, 1988; Mayer and Kosmin, 1994), but some countervailing efforts and trends are also visible.

Marriage and family formation through the addition of children are looked upon favorably by all ethnic groups. Alternative forms, such as living together without marriage, same-sex committed relationships, and singleness-by-choice tend to be viewed as deviations from tradition, sometimes as disloyalty to ethnic group membership, and therefore they are often met with suspicion if not outright hostility on the part of older generations.

Ethnic lenses contain a lining, as it were, or a framework of tradition. The history of the ethnic group is important and older people are seen as the bearers, sometimes as the creators, of that history. Partly for that reason, older persons are viewed with much greater respect and reverence than is the case in the broader American community. Not only are they more likely to involve themselves in decisions made by younger family members, but their blessing is often sought actively by the younger members. This sometimes leaves a perception on the part of people outside the group that members of ethnic groups are less independent, less autonomous, or perhaps less mature than they should be for their age. In fact, there is no evidence for this point of view. The younger adult members of the group are simply acting according to their ethnic group norms, doing what their reference group and their community considers to be right and proper in giving weight to the opinions and points of view of older group members.

Ethnic group norms generally favor keeping aging and aged family members in a family context. Ending life, including literally dying, at home is often seen as proper. Warehousing aged family members in institutional settings, often nonethnic in content and context, is viewed as disrespectful to tradition, inhumane to the aged person, and uncharacteristic of the ethnic group. This is not to say that institutionalized care is never necessary, by any means, but rather to underscore the painful feelings which accompany such a step on the part of a family.

Social Work Practice with Families

These sketches and comments on family ethnicity point in some interesting directions if one is concerned with relevant and effective social work practice. The first is that family treatment—efforts that involve more than one, and usually several, family members in efforts to change—is highly indicated. As the family plays such an important part for its members in ethnic communities, change efforts that do not involve the family seem frequently doomed to failure. In a patriarchal structure such as is found in many Asian-American families, it may be vital to involve the father in counseling or treatment. Lum (1992) quotes Ruiz and Padilla as stating that "family therapies probably yield higher success rates among Hispanic Americans than among non-Hispanic Americans, regardless of whether the problem is intrapsychic or extrapsychic" (p. 42).

Group work should often be the modality of choice, whether the group is made up entirely of members of a particular ethnic group or whether a mixture of ethnic identities with other ethnics or with nonethnic identified members characterizes the group composition. The ethnic world is an interpersonal one. Learning, teaching, comparing, and weighing the advice of others is a part of the ethnic tradition. Groups lend themselves to such learning processes.

Conversely, accepting an "expert" point of view, especially from someone one does not know and someone with whom one does not share ethnic group membership is often *not* part of the ethnic group tradition. Social workers should be aware that what is often expected of "good" clients flies in the face of ethnic group norms and traditions. Finding ways of involving others—family members, other ethnic group members, or others whose life experiences and points of view are compatible—is a way to normalize the social work client status for many ethnic group members. Doing so may raise issues ranging from confidentiality to changing the normative ways a social agency operates. Serious thought devoted to these issues will result in more effective and efficient services to ethnic group members. Ignoring and showing insensitivity to these issues will simply result in the ethnic community's perception of an agency or service as belonging to "them" rather than to "us," leading the ethnic community to avoid or resist using that agency.

Working Through the Ethnic Lens

We use the concept of an ethnic lens as a metaphor and model in this book. When working with families, whether with the entire family or with one or more individuals within a family context, the ethnic lens can become quite real. It takes on reality from the variance between the ways that social workers, and sometimes their agencies, see the nature of problems and the ways that family members, and sometimes the family as a whole, understand them. At times it seems as though the two are looking at the world literally through different lenses.

Schwartz's (1961) concept that one of the worker's important functions is to help the participants search out and identify "the common ground" applies also, in our view, to work with families. Clearly, there will be differences between the family's view and that of a social worker. The question is, can enough commonality be found, established, and identified to make it clear that there is a basis for reciprocal and cooperative work? This is a crucial test of the worker's skill in working with an ethnic family.

The other implication that seems clear to us is the need to involve various family members earlier, more deeply, and perhaps longer than may be the case with other kinds of families. To be sure, this raises issues of confidentiality, and such involvement needs to be discussed with the identified client, if this is how intervention began. But the skill of mobilizing a family on behalf of one of its members, like the skill of mobilizing a community on behalf of one of its members, is important and, in some instances, spells the difference between success and failure in providing the help that the family members came seeking from the social worker.

Questions for Discussion

1. Identify five aspects of ethnic families that you would explore with a client during the initial (intake-and-assessment) phase of treatment.

2. Why does ethnic identity make such a difference to members of an ethnic family, and how should a social worker respond if she or he is not the same ethnicity as the client family?
3. Compare and contrast two strategies for helping ethnic parents take a look at the outcome of their child-rearing techniques, giving the strengths and weakness of both.
4. Why do some families choose to obtain help and services exclusively from a sectarian agency and others choose not to?
5. Would you be more likely to recommend or undertake family treatment with members of one ethnicity than another?

References

Adorno, T. W., Frenkel-Brunswich, E., Levinson, D. J., and Sanford, R. N. (1950). *The Authoritarian Personality*. New York: Harper and Brothers.

Alba, R. D. (1990). *Ethnic Identity: The Transformation of White America*. New Haven, CT: Yale University Press.

Chilman, C. S. (1993). Hispanic families in the United States: Research perspectives. In H. P. McAdoo (Ed.), *Family Ethnicity: Strength in Diversity* (pp. 141–163). Newbury Park, CA: Sage.

DiBlasio, F. A. (1993). Helping family members to forgive: Role of social workers' religious beliefs. *Families in Society*, *74*, 163–170.

Enright, R. D., and the Human Development Study Group (1991). The moral development of forgiveness. In W. Kurtines and J. Gewirtz (Eds.). *Handbook of Moral Behavior and Development*, Vol. 1 (pp. 123–152). Hillsdale, NJ: Erlbaum.

Glick, P. C. (1988). Demographic pictures of Black families. In H. P. McAdoo (Ed.), *Black Families* (2nd ed., pp. 111–132). Newbury Park, CA: Sage.

Lum, D. (1992). *Social Work Practice and People of Color: A Process-Stage Approach*, (2nd ed.). Monterey, CA: Brooks/Cole.

Mayer, E., and Kosmin, B. (1994). *National Survey of Religious Identification*. New York: City University of New York.

McAdoo, H. P. (Ed.). (1993). *Family Ethnicity: Strength in Diversity.* Newbury Park, CA: Sage.

McAdoo, J. L. (1993). Decision making and marital satisfaction in African American families. In H. P. McAdoo (Ed.), *Family Ethnicity: Strength in Diversity* (pp. 109–119). Newbury Park, CA: Sage.

Mindel, C. H., and Habenstein, R. W. (Eds.). (1976). *Ethnic Families in America: Patterns and Variations*. New York: Elsevier Science.

Nanji, A. A. (1993). The Muslim family in North America: Continuity and change (pp. 229–242). In H. P. McAdoo (ed.). *Family Ethnicity: Strength in Diversity*. Newbury Park, CA: Sage.

Schwartz, W. (1961). The social worker in the group. In *New Perspectives on Services to Groups: Theory, Organization, and Practice*. New York: National Association of Social Workers.

Worthington, E. (Ed.). (1993). *Psychotherapy and Religious Values*. Grand Rapids, MI: Baker Book House.

Wood, G. G., and Middleman, R. R. (1989). *The Structural Approach to Direct Practice in Social Work*. New York: Columbia University Press.

5

Ethnicity and Communities

Social work's role among the helping professions is unique in that it is not restricted to the individual, the family, or even the group. The ecological perspective for practice emphasizes the interaction of people with their environments, underscoring the fact that people do not live in vacuums and that their interactions with their relationships and environments are significant factors in their well-being. Ethnicity, as a primary characteristic of the environments or communities in which people live, is a major component of these interactions. Assuring that communities are supportive to individual and group functioning is a primary social work task, which traces its roots to the earliest days of the profession.

Community boundaries can be rigid, in that they permit little interaction of residents with those outside, or pliant, with community residents having easy access to the greater society. Communities also differ according to their resources and their ability to meet residents' needs. Formal resources such as institutions and services that form the structure of communities are needed for meeting economic needs, while informal resources, particularly social networks and organizations, are necessary for meeting social and emotional needs.

Ethnicity may act as a boundary separating ethnic groups from the greater society. Communities with rigid boundaries will show stronger adherence to traditional values and norms as they engage in less interaction with the greater society. Within the community boundaries, social roles and behaviors are shaped according to the specific culture. To the extent that these roles and behaviors strongly diverge from those outside of the community, interactions with the greater society are likely to be stressful.

Ethnic communities, in contrast to mainstream America, often maintain high levels of mutual support and responsibility, and a collective outlook among residents (Beulah, Madsen, Sullivan, Swindler, and Tipton, 1985). These characteristics strengthen the commitment, unity, and ethnic solidarity of community residents, and they also act as major resources for social well-being. These resources are particularly critical when residents are deprived of the rewards available to other members of society. Thus, within the community, individuals who are devalued through society's lens can achieve self-esteem and status. In this way, the ethnic community can be a source of strength to its residents, counteracting the negative effects that frequently result from persons' interactions with the greater society.

A vivid example of the stress that relations with society can engender is shown in a study of the mental health of Mexican Americans in Los Angeles (Burnam, Hough, Karno, Escobar, and Telles, 1987). In this instance, assimilation was found to have negative effects on well-being, in that the more highly Americanized the immigrant, the poorer the mental health. This poorer health was associated with lower levels of self-esteem stemming from the stress of attempting to assimilate to a society that presents barriers to integration.

Solidarity and identification within ethnic communities are dependent upon the degrees of "assertion and accommodation" of the residents (Woldemikael, 1987). Assertion is the process by which persons resist new cultural or institutional relationships, while accommodation is the process by which individuals submit to these relationships. Using assertion, groups struggle to maintain their traditions, while, through accommodation, groups seek to adapt.

Refugees who have had to flee their native countries are more likely to stress assertion as they seek to maintain their culture in the new country. Immigrants who came willingly to the country tend to be more interested in accommodation and assimilating into the new society. However, given this dichotomy, it is important to recognize that many groups may be perceived as assertive due to the exclusionary behavior of a society that works to keep them out.

An understanding of the reasons for assertion or accommodation is critical for the clarity of the ethnic lens and for effective social work practice. For example, knowing whether groups live within specific neighborhoods or use ethnic agencies through preference or due to discriminatory practices will influence the role, actions, and credibility of the community worker. Groups preferring assertion of their own traditional ways of life will resent efforts towards integration. Indeed, strong actions on the part of the worker to promote accommodation may actually undermine any efforts at further involvement with the ethnic community.

Community Typologies and Ethnicity

Communities are formed when a group of people create a social unit based on common location, interest, identification, culture, and activities (Garvin and Tropman, 1992). Communities of identification (Longres, 1990) are based on some specific feature or common identity or belief such as race, religion, lifestyle, ideology, sexual orientation, social class, profession, or type of employment. These persons often live in locality-based communities, residential areas that have high proportions of persons sharing specific characteristics (Fellin, 1995). Examples of locality-based communities on ethnic background include the Chinese, Korean, Jewish, and Italian neighborhoods that exist in many cities.

Predominantly gay areas, such as West Hollywood in Los Angeles or the Castro in San Francisco, are examples of locality-based communities that reflect particular lifestyles or ideologies. As the communities are based on salient characteristics of the group members, they are often considered ethnic.

Many persons living outside of a designated community, but who closely identify with its ethnic traditions, characteristics, or residents, may in fact consider themselves community members. These persons often become actively involved in the community or act as its advocates when it appears to be threatened or is undergoing change. As an example, the development of a major highway through an established ethnic community can provoke widespread community action by ethnic group members who, although no longer living in the designated area, maintain a strong allegiance to it. In this way, community membership can supersede the recognized neighborhood boundaries.

For those living outside of the area, ethnic communities offer a visible link to an identity that is lost in the greater society. Ethnic neighborhoods are important as visible manifestations of this identity, as well as for their capacity to concentrate the institutions and cultures of an ethnic group, thereby keeping alive the sentiments and loyalties associated with ethnicity in adult residents and acting as a major mechanism for socializing a new generation to ethnic ways (Breton, 1964). Restaurants, markets, festivals, and shops serve to reinforce cultural traditions and help to assure their continuation.

Community Functions

It is through local services and institutions within communities that individual and group needs are met. Warren (1963) defines the five pivotal functions performed by communities and necessary for the effective functioning of the residents as production/distribution/consumption, socialization, social control, social participation, and social support. Schools, police, hospitals, social service agencies, banks, stores, self-help groups, and other informal groups are among the institutions that carry out these functions.

Ethnicity, particularly as it is often closely linked with resources, is an important factor in these institutions. Ethnicity can determine both the character of institutions and the ways in which functions are carried out. Ethnic communities with rigid boundaries and little positive interaction with the greater society often struggle to meet the residents' needs. An absence of jobs in inner cities, lower levels of education of community members, and fewer applicable skills restrict both production and consumption. The functioning of residents is often further impeded by feelings of apathy and fear as crime becomes common. Frequently, institutions, such as schools and hospitals, within these areas are poorly equipped to meet the needs of the population.

The socialization of children into the values of the greater society is difficult within communities where institutional functions are not adequately performed. Anger and distrust, coupled with discrimination and deprivation, impede accommodation. At the same time, children socialized into the ethnic community, learning it roles and modes of behavior, are vulnerable to stressful interactions with those outside of the community whose patterns of behavior differ. Social control pertains to the forces within the community that determine residents' behavior, assuring that they behave according to established community norms. Local government agencies such as the courts and the police are formal mechanisms of control, while families and individuals act as informal controls.

Ethnic communities vary with regard to the social control function. Established communities in which people tend to remain and which engender strong feelings of allegiance are likely to have greater control of the residents than are newer, more mobile communities. As an example, within the Orthodox Jewish community of Brooklyn, New York, informal social control through families and relationships is a powerful determinant of persons' behaviors and relationships, including the selection of marriage partners.

Social participation can be informal through networks of family and friends or formal through institutions such as schools, churches, and clubs. Local ethnic organizations, clubs, and family activities are frequent sources of social participation for community members. Within many ethnic communities, social participation is strong within these local groups, while participation within the larger community remains limited.

Familial and informal ties within ethnic communities form the basis for strong social support systems. These supports are critical in assisting residents with economic and family problems and in times of illness. Such informal support systems can be the primary source of help, with individuals turning toward formal supports such as social services only when these informal supports are depleted or nonexistent.

Communities practice aims to assure that the environments in which people live are nurturing and contain the essential resources and supports that permit these functions to occur. These aims, which seek to improve community functioning, are based on the following assumptions (Solomon, 1985):

1. Dysfunctional communities are those that do not provide adequate resources to support effective social functioning of its residents.
2. Minority communities are less functional than other communities due to institutional inequities, which limit access to resources. Because resources translate into power, these communities are therefore essentially powerless.
3. There is a reciprocal relationship between individuals and communities. That is, functional communities support individual growth while functional individuals support community growth. Conversely, dysfunctional communities do not support individual growth while dysfunctional individuals do not support community growth.
4. Community social work practice in minority communities is aimed at reducing powerlessness of the community's residents to act collectively. This involves assessing and coping with institutional inequities.

Ethnic Minority Communities

Gemeinschaft refers to a social system based upon relationships that are personal, informal, traditional, general, and sentimental (Toennies, 1961). Conversely, *gesellschaft* is a social system characterized by impersonal, contractual, utilitarian, and specialized relationships. These concepts are particularly applicable to the description of ethnic minority communities.

Ethnic minority communities with strong internal support systems are classified as *neo-gemeinschaft* in that the cultural, social, political, and economic relationships occurring within them are major determinants of daily life (Rivera and Erlich, 1984). The communities are "new" in that they consist of specific groups coming together in a new country or area where they attempt to continue their traditions in a hostile environment.

Rivera and Erlich offer the following structural characteristics of neo-gemeinshaft ethnic minority communities: They are relatively homogeneous; English is not often spoken; there is a shared experience of racism and oppression; these are many extended family networks; decision making is usually by consensus, with little trust of outside power; there are strong feelings of alienation and anomie by the leaders; there is a marginal-to-poor level of existence, with welfare a constant reality; there are ethnic signs, newspapers, and flavors; and there exist strong social networks.

Social networks are particularly important in new ethnic communities, as those arriving are frequently without other ties. Many have been forced to emigrate due to economic, political, or social turmoil in their native countries. The information, practical assistance, contacts, and orientation to the new society offered by networks are major sources of support and integration into the new society.

Communities can be particularly important for ethnic minorities because they can offer resources necessary for survival denied them by the greater society. Taylor (1979), in his discussion of black communities, describes minority neighborhoods as both spatial and sociopsychological communities. As southern blacks migrated to the North, they settled in predominantly segregated neighborhoods. Within these neighborhoods, spatial communities, they developed their own institutions and networks, which have offered resources and assistance often not available elsewhere. Moreover, as these bonds serve both to unite members within the community and to maintain their distinctness from those outside, they act as sociopsychological communities offering emotional support to the residents.

Ghettos are sections within urban areas that have extremely high concentrations of ethnic group members. In the United States, ghettos have been primarily associated with African Americans living in poverty, with inadequate housing and poor social conditions. Unemployment, female-headed families, and a high proportion of persons dependent on welfare characterize ghetto residents. In many areas, communities have deteriorated as manufacturing jobs have been lost and replaced by an upsurge in part-time, low-paying work, causing the conditions of these ghettos to worsen (Wacquant and Wilson, 1993).

In their study of ghetto residents in Chicago, Wacquant and Wilson describe today's ghettos as primarily composed of the most marginal and oppressed sections of the black community. Comparing the residents with low-income blacks living outside of the ghetto, they find that the residents suffer socially as well as economically. They are more likely to be unmarried, less likely to have close friends, less likely to belong to organizations, and less likely to know their neighbors. As the area becomes increasingly poor, unemployed residents with few connections to employment or ties outside of the ghetto are further isolated. In the period 1970–1980, Chicago experienced a growth in poverty in the inner city caused by the increase in numbers of minority teenagers and young adults lacking skills and education and the simultaneous departure of upwardly mobile minorities (Wilson, 1987). The community thus becomes further isolated from society.

With these economic and social restrictions, ghetto residents remain structurally trapped within their community. Their cultural isolation, the lack of resources, and the absence of jobs can foster attitudes and behaviors that in themselves further restrict the ability of residents to interact with those outside of the ghetto's boundaries. At the same time, the frustrations of residents can erupt in anger and riots as residents find themselves confined and deprived of the means of reaching the goals and rewards available to others in society.

Refugee and Immigrant Communities

In examining ethnic communities and their adaptation experiences, Gold (1992) distinguishes between the experiences of refugees and immigrants. Because of their shared plight, refugees are more likely to be unified in communities than are immigrants. The latter are more likely to come to this country on a voluntary basis and out of individual motivations rather than due to fears of persecution.

The forces propelling refugees to leave their homelands often mean that they have little time to prepare for their departure, are able to take less capital and assets, and must depart in order to survive. These negative forces can foster an adherence to traditional values and roles and a sense of responsibility for maintaining a culture that may be threatened. The same forces can also act as a basis for refugees' political involvement. The Cuban community in Miami, "Little Havana," exemplifies a refugee community that has maintained strong traditions while also becoming a basis for collective political action.

In contrast, the Vietnamese and Soviet Jewish refugee populations in the United States are diverse and segmented, with ethnic solidarity occurring only at a very local level (Gold,1992). Diverse backgrounds, classes, ideologies, religious outlooks, and regions have kept these groups from becoming collectively organized communities. Mutual suspicion, class and occupational differences, religion, and political and regional differences act as barriers to the development of community ties, networks, and a solid political base.

Solidarity among the three subgroups within the Vietnamese population—the South Vietnamese elite who entered the United States before 1975, the more recently arrived "boat people," who were predominantly working class, and the ethnic Chinese—is difficult to establish (Rumbaut, 1989; Skinner, 1980). Socioeconomic and ethnic distinctions between these groups act as barriers within communities, preventing a sense of commonality. Such barriers are difficult for outsiders to perceive but must be understood when working with community residents.

In recent years, with new waves of immigration to the United States, the number and diversity of ethnic minority communities has increased. At the same time, even established communities, whose members originally came early in this century, have become greatly enlarged by new waves of immigrants. For example, waves of immigrants from Laos, Thailand, and Cambodia have increased the heterogeneity of the Asian-American population, while Latino communities now include many immigrants and refugees from Nicaragua, El Salvador, and Cuba. Although these groups may share many characteristics, their varying backgrounds and experiences can prevent them from unifying into a solid community. Unfortunately, the ethnic lens of the practitioner often fails to perceive the group differences.

Immigrant communities often develop in inner-city neighborhoods, where living is cheaper but economic opportunities and resources are scarce. In order to succeed, these emerging communities must carve out their own niches in the labor market and free enterprise system (Daley and Wong, 1994). Korean grocers, Pakistani taxi drivers, and Latino service workers are examples of occupations frequently taken by these newer immigrants. But, with scarce opportunities, tensions and rivalries within neighborhoods frequently develop, as ethnic groups compete for employment and resources. In the extreme, this competition can result in violence, as occurred in the 1993 Los Angeles riots, when many Korean businesses in African-American neighborhoods were attacked and burned.

Community Needs

Communities are often characterized according to their needs, whether they be better roads, schools, education, health care, or services. Such needs may be determined by governing officials, local agencies, or residents themselves. Identifying needs and working toward meeting them, comparable to work with individuals, form a basis for much community work.

Zastrow (1995) differentiates among four types of needs. *Felt needs* are those that individuals themselves perceive, such as needs for clean water and safe parks. *Expressed needs* are those that individuals share with others, such as the need for better schools. *Prescribed needs* are needs that an expert perceives as necessary, but that are not necessarily recognized by the community. Finally, *comparative needs* are noticed when one community is found to be lacking in services or amenities found in another community, such as police patrols or garbage collection.

In working with communities, social workers must begin with what the residents themselves perceive as important or needed. Working with residents to meet felt and expressed needs provides the basis for further community work. In fact, efforts to meet proscribed or comparative needs that are not experienced as urgent by residents can seriously threaten the credibility of the worker or program, placing further efforts at risk. The design of community programs and their goals must be congruent with what residents themselves perceive as important.

Example

> In a small rural southern community, Department of Housing and Urban Development (HUD) money was used to develop single-family homes in a new area for low-income minority persons living in very inadequate housing, often with no plumbing or heat.
>
> However, to the surprise of the local government officials and builders, persons were reluctant to purchase these homes. Underlying this reluctance were the residents' suspicions of government-funded programs, which in the past had offered promises that had not been fulfilled. In addition, most intended residents were living in houses and in areas that had been in their family for several generations. Within these areas were extensive kinship and informal networks that offered strong emotional and instrumental support.
>
> Had the social planners perceived the community through a clearer ethnic lens, rather than one that reflected back onto themselves, they could have concentrated their funds on improving the housing in the existing community instead of developing a new neighborhood. This type of effort would both meet the needs of the residents and establish the credibility and sensitivity of the local government to those needs.

Community Development and Empowerment

Community development involves "efforts made by professionals and community residents to enhance the social bonds among members of the community, motivate the citizens for self-help, develop responsible local leadership, and create or vitalize local institutions" (Barker, 1991, p. 43). The development process involves promoting the participation of the community residents and the provision of technical assistance to foster leadership development. Development, to a large part, rests upon the skills and ability of residents to improve their conditions.

Empowerment is a term used to describe the collective political power of groups to effect change (Fagan, 1979). Empowerment at the group level involves an awareness of how political structures affect individual and group experiences, thus permitting individuals and groups to see that problems result from a lack of power. They can therefore focus on changing the causes of the problems. Involved in the process is the reduction of self-blame so that persons no longer feel responsible for their situations. They are also able to assume personal responsibility for future change.

Central to empowerment is involving the client, whether individual, group, or community, as an equal partner in the change process. At the individual level, this requires the worker to be a partner, rather than the authority, in the change process. Actively involving the client fosters a sense of power and control. At the community level, empowerment means that community members are given the authority to make decisions and choices, with the worker facilitating the development of the knowledge and resources necessary for making these choices (Zippay, 1995). Zippay describes three approaches to the use of empowerment in communities. Each has been used frequently among ethnic minority populations.

The first approach is strengthening internal resources, based upon attitudinal adjustment, as the key factor for social change. An example is the "Just Say No" campaign, which focused on self-help through willpower and community participation.

The second approach to community empowerment emphasizes individual choice and internal capacity building which includes the control of external forces. Promoting home ownership by low-income people through increasing their ability to purchase low-income housing while controlling mortgage rates and penalties is an example. This approach encourages self-help, thus reducing dependency.

Creating community partnerships between poor and low-income communities to solve problems such as drug abuse, joblessness, and high school dropout is another approach to empowerment. It entails the involvement of public officials, institutional leaders, community-based organizations, and neighborhood residents in the self-help efforts. At the same time, the outside agencies provide training in leadership and resource development.

As these examples illustrate, empowerment within minority communities is a complex process involving interventions at both the micro and macro levels of practice. Empowerment cannot be accomplished without raising individual self-esteem, teaching new skills and behaviors, developing resources, and establishing a basis for political power within the community.

Empowerment is a means to altering the lens through which ethnic minority persons perceive themselves and their communities. By developing skills and abilities and experiencing change, their own beliefs and attitudes, and consequently the way in which they see themselves and others, can be changed. Empowerment can alter the perception of being a victim in a hopeless situation.

Within ethnic agencies, those agencies providing services to their own ethnic group, empowerment is a basis for practice (Inglehart and Becerra, 1995). These agencies, with their ethnic staff, personify the ability of the group to control and develop their own programs. Moreover, staff themselves are empowered as they take on new roles and activities and assist other members of the community. Clients are empowered as they see role models from their own ethnic group. The new information and skills learned through the agency reinforce the empowerment, which can then be utilized in addressing various community problems.

Framework for Practice in Ethnic Communities

Social works' involvement in community work can take many forms, ranging from organizing residents to developing programs and services within the community. Among the activities of these practitioners are fund raising, lobbying, developing group and leadership skills, assisting local services, planning interorganizational activities, and advocating for residents.

The skills needed for these tasks are similar to those needed in work with individuals and groups. Workers must be able to engage community members by establishing trusting relationships. The credibility that forms a basis for these relationships will, to a large degree, be influenced by the ethnic sensitivity of the worker.

Comparable to practice with individual ethnic clients, social workers in macro practice must be knowledgeable about the background of the community and its experiences in order to develop appropriate objectives and interventions. In particular, workers must have an understanding of the institutions and services within the community and the accessibility to residents of outside services. Workers must be knowledgeable about the extent to which existing programs and services actually meet the needs of the residents.

The specific types of data needed for work with ethnic communities can be categorized in eight items.

1. GEOGRAPHY AND POPULATION CONCENTRATION

The geography of a community pertains to its physical boundaries, which are not always clearly visible to an outsider. Many ethnic communities are clustered around a distinct neighborhood with ethnic churches, shops, and restaurants. The boundaries around these centralized areas may be very distinct, due to heavy concentration of ethnic group members.

However, many ethnic communities spread beyond designated boundaries as persons move outside of the area but continue to identify with the community and its residents. Consequently, actions and development efforts within the community will be most effective if they include links with these "outsiders." In fact, because these persons bridge both the greater society and the more traditional community they can be significant contributors to the development efforts.

Census data can be helpful in locating African-American, Hispanic, and Asian communities, but they are of little help in identifying other ethnic concentrations. Becoming familiar with neighborhoods, walking through them, and talking with community persons—"insiders" who are members of the ethnic population—are ways of learning about the boundaries of the community and improving the acuity of the ethnic lens.

2. COMMUNITY PROBLEMS, NEEDS, CONCERNS

Understanding the ways in which community residents perceive problems and their perceptions of needs and pressing concerns is the basis for community work. As discussed earlier, addressing proscribed and comparative needs prior to felt and expressed needs can doom the change efforts and the credibility of the worker. If problems addressed are not considered relevant by the groups or are even inappropriate for the specific ethnic community, efforts are bound to fail (Rivera and Erlich, 1992).

A frequently used technique for identifying community needs is a needs assessment. Needs assessments collect information about problems within a given community and are often used for service planning and the allocation of resources. Indicators such as the demand for medical or social services in an area provide a picture of the community, while surveys of agencies show the specific types of services they offer and the demands they cannot meet. These methods offer a picture of needs that can be enhanced by community members.

Techniques for obtaining the perspectives of community residents include surveys, community meetings, talks with key community individuals, and focus groups. Each of these methods can give the practitioner a perspective on what the local residents perceive as the most pressing needs and issues. Depending upon time and resources, the use of any one method in conjunction with another can provide a comprehensive perspective of residents' views of needs. As an example, in planning for mental health services within a community, a community meeting may generate important discussion and information on the views of individuals regarding mental health services. Focus groups can be used to assist in clarifying the specific types of problems residents have and their anticipated responses to a service.

3. DEGREE OF HOMOGENEITY OF ETHNIC GROUP

Homogeneity pertains to the social stratification of the residents, the social classes to which they belong and with which they identify. An important factor in homogeneity is the extent to which residents identify with each other and share similar backgrounds and experiences. As an example, among the Vietnamese communities the heterogeneity of the residents is often quite diverse, due to their social classes, years in this country, and places of origin in Vietnam.

This heterogeneity can be an obstacle to community solidarity and subsequent development efforts. Thus, services appropriate for one segment of the community may be irrelevant to or even conflict with the values or needs of another segment. Moreover, if animosity exists among community groups, programs designed to serve the entire community may remain underutilized because individuals are reluctant to interact with each other.

4. COMMUNITY RESOURCES—BUSINESSES, ETHNIC ORGANIZATIONS, SUPPORT NETWORKS

The economic and social viability of the community is determined to a large extent by its resources. Having many businesses within the community that are owned by local residents can be a major source of income as well as ethnic identity and pride. Organizations and support networks that provide mutual help and promote a sense of identity indicate self-reliance within the ethnic community. The stronger these organizations and the more they meet the needs of community members, the less interest persons will have in the interventions of an outsider. As an example, in many communities, grassroots organizations focusing on specific issues, such as safe streets, drug abuse by children, and developing local businesses, have become major social institutions. Consequently, the need for outsiders and their efforts is sharply diminished.

Organizations can be vital links to the community. Having persons from organizations on program boards, involved in planning efforts, and representing the project to others in the community is critical for eliciting support within the community. Local organizations and groups give credibility to the practitioner or agency seeking to work in the ethnic community. The involvement of the Parent Teacher Association (PTA) in an afterschool program being established for young adolescents can be instrumental in assuring community members that the program is reputable and that the organizers can be trusted.

5. VALUES, TRADITIONS, ATTITUDES TOWARD NONMEMBERS

Practitioners must be knowledgeable about the ways in which nonmembers and their efforts at involvement are perceived. Knowing whether the values and traditions of the ethnic group view such efforts as intrusive and with suspicion or whether members are open and receptive to such involvement is critical.

Knowledge of the group's previous experiences with outsiders or development plans is also important for understanding attitudes and responses. Apathy or hostility could be due to previous negative experiences with planners or social workers, expectations that were not realized, or traditional distrust of any outsider. Depending upon the reasons underlying the negative attitudes, workers will first either have to establish trust and credibility or demonstrate why their interests and goals are compatible with those of the community.

Residents may also be suspicious of nonmembers if they have information that they are concerned about concealing. Worries about immigration status can be major factors affecting the willingness to use services. Attributing reticence or reluctance regarding services to apathy or cultural values can ignore the political realities facing the group members. The clear ethnic lens must be able to discern values and attitudes from worries and tensions regarding possible deportation.

6. COMMUNITY LEADERS

Workers need to understand the qualities associated with leadership in the community, to identify the community leaders, and to encourage their involvement. These leaders are persons whom residents respect and trust and who often wield considerable power and influence. Such leaders may be educators, members of the clergy, media personalities, or businesspersons. Leadership may actually have little relation to the person's present role. Often it is primarily dependent upon the person's role or status in the native country. In addition, the characteristics associated with leadership frequently differ among ethnic groups, as different traits are held in esteem. For example, within the Orthodox Jewish community, leadership tends to be associated with religious scholarship, while among the Vietnamese, leaders are frequently those who were military heroes in Vietnam.

Identifying and involving community notables in the project can help to assure social workers' credibility. Similar to the involvement of organizations, involving leaders in a project acts as a link to the community (Cox, 1987). As respected notables are legitimated by the local community, they can be influential in the acceptance of the worker and the project. At the same time, practitioners must be cautious about involving persons who are not respected within the community. To do so can seriously undermine the project and the worker.

7. DEGREE OF ASSERTION OR ACCOMMODATION

Residents who are concerned with maintaining ethnic traditions and community cohesiveness are likely to resist involvement with outsiders, which can be perceived as threatening to ethnic values and the community's viability. As noted earlier, this is often the case with refugees, who are more likely than immigrants to be assertive in their desire to maintain the traditions associated with the country they were forced to leave. Understanding the perspective of the community with regard to assertion or accommodation is critical, as it will strongly influence responses to the practitioner.

8. DEGREE OF VISIBLE ETHNIC LINKS

Ethnic media (newspapers and radio stations), restaurants, stores, and other services are visible links with traditions and serve as sources of cultural identity for community members as well as for those living outside of the community boundaries. Numerous ethnic links suggest that cultural values and ties are strong within the community and that ethnicity is a salient characteristic of the residents. Conversely, few ethnic links may indicate that the community is attempting to integrate into the larger society and that persons no longer attempt to distinguish themselves from others.

When links are visible, they can assist practitioners in overcoming barriers into the community. As an example, the ethnic media can be a source of support and entry into the community. Many individuals, regardless of their level of assimilation, listen to the radio, watch television, and read newspapers in their native language. Using the media to describe projects or plans can assist in disseminating information throughout the community. The media can increase residents' understanding of a project and elicit their involvement, acceptance, and participation.

The Ethnic Lens

Effective work with ethnic communities is dependent upon the clarity of the lenses of both the practitioner and the community residents. In the first instance, the lens must be sensitive to the boundaries of the community and the saliency of its values and traditions, its institutions, and its leaders. In the second instance, community members must perceive the practitioner as trustworthy and sensitive to their needs and concerns.

Effective community work depends upon social workers being able to bridge the gap between their perspectives of the world and those of the community members. It necessitates a multicultural consciousness and knowledge about the community's value systems and problem-solving behaviors (Glugoski, Reisch, and Rivera, 1994).

The lens of the practitioner must be able to identify accurately the needs and priorities of residents. As discussed earlier, there are many available strategies that can assist in this assessment and identification process. Proceeding without them can undermine organizing efforts, for then the concerns of the practitioner are not congruent with those of the community.

As in other work with ethnic populations, community workers must be aware of their own values and beliefs, particularly with regard to community relationships, behaviors, and structures and the ways these can affect their perceptions and actions. As an example, workers accustomed to formal relationships within communities and restricted contacts between neighbors may find it difficult to understand communities that are dependent on extensive informal relationships and networks. Such communities may appear to be disorganized and unstructured and, consequently, practitioners may see their role as organizing persons into formal systems. These efforts are unlikely to succeed, for they fail to recognize the importance of these informal ties. In this instance, the lens is reflecting back upon the perceiver.

Generalizations are a source of distortion because they fail to recognize the heterogeneity that may exist within the ethnic community. The lens must be able to discern the importance of factors such as class differences and backgrounds, which can affect present relationships and the ability of members to work together toward common goals. Not being able to perceive the differences among residents can further undermine the practitioner's efforts.

In working with ethnic communities, social workers must be sensitive to the lens through which the residents perceive them. As discussed earlier, persons in communities with rigid boundaries, those with few interactions with outsiders, or those who have had negative experiences with the greater society are likely to view workers cynically, as intrusive, or with suspicion. Knowledge of the political realities affecting groups, such as concern over their immigration status, is essential since it can be a major determinant of acceptance and involvement.

At the same time, new immigrants are often unfamiliar with grassroots activities or organizations. Those coming from totalitarian countries are unlikely to have had any experience in community groups as a means of democratically expressing their concerns and needs. Moreover, any experiences they may have had are likely to have been with groups sponsored by the government itself, with activities closely monitored. Through their lenses, community workers are likely to be perceived as government agents whose motives cannot be trusted. Establishing trust and credibility and clarifying the purpose of the organization and the roles of the leader and community members is critical for community practice.

Finally, the success of social workers in ethnic communities will depend upon the relationships that are established with the residents and the links that they develop with the community. These relationships help to assure that both the lens of the practitioner and that of the ethnic community are as clear as possible. Involving persons and organizations in the project from its earliest stage helps to insure that its aims and objectives, as well as the means of reaching them, are congruent with community values and traditions.

Questions for Discussion

1. Describe the factors that can contribute to solidarity within ethnic communities and the impact that solidarity can have on group members' lives.
2. Discuss the characteristics of a ghetto and how living in a ghetto can affect its residents.

3. Explain the differences between immigrant and refugee communities.
4. What factors need to be considered in encouraging community empowerment?
5. Explain the limitations of relying on census data in identifying ethnic communities.

References

Barker, R. (1991). *The Social Work Dictionary* (2nd ed.). Silver Spring, MD: National Association of Social Workers.

Beulah, R., Madsen, R., Sullivan, W., Swidler, A., and Tipton, S. (1985). *Habits of the Heart: Individualism and Commitment in American Life.* Berkeley, CA: University of California Press.

Breton, R. (1964) Institutional completeness of ethnic communities and the personal relations of immigrants. *American Journal of Sociology, 70,* 193–205.

Burnam, A., Hough, R., Karno, M., Escobar, J., and Telles, C. (1987). Acculaturation and lifetime prevalence of psychiatric disorders among Mexican Americans in Los Angeles. *Journal of Health and Social Behavior, 28,* 89–102.

Cox, C. (1987). Overcoming access problems in ethnic communities. In D. Gelfand and C. Barresi (Eds.), *Ethnic Dimensions in Aging* (pp. 165–178). New York: Springer.

Daley, J., and Wong, P. (1994). Community development with emerging ethnic communities. *Journal of Community Practice, 1,* 9–24.

Fagan, H. (1979). *Empowerment: Skills for Parish Social Work.* New York: Paulist Press.

Fellin, P. (1995). Understanding American communities. In J. Rothman, J. Ehrlich, and J. Tropman (Eds.) *Strategies of Community Intervention* (pp. 114–128). Itasca, IL: F. E. Peacock.

Garvin, C., and Tropman, J. (1992). *Social Work in Contemporary Society.* Englewood Cliffs, NJ: Prentice Hall.

Glugoski, G., Reisch, M., and Rivera, F. (1994). A wholistic ethno-cultural paradigm: A new model for community organization teaching and practice. *Journal of Community Practice, 1,* 81–98.

Gold, S. (1992). *Refugee Communities: A Comparative Field Study.* Newbury Park, CA: Sage.

Green, J. (1982). *Cultural Awareness in the Human Services.* Englewood Cliffs, NJ: Prentice Hall.

Inglehart, A., and Becerra, R. (1995). *Social Services and the Ethnic Community.* Boston: Allyn and Bacon.

Longres, J. (1990). *Human Behavior and the Social Environment.* Itasca, IL: F. E. Peacock.

Rivera, R., and Erlich, J. (1984). An assessment framework for organizing in emerging minority communities. In F. Cox, J. Erlich, J. Rothman, and J. Tropman (Eds.), *Tactics and Techniques of Community Practice* (2nd ed., pp. 98–108). Itasca, IL: F. E. Peacock.

Rivera, R., and Erlich, J. (1992). *Community Organizing in a Diverse Society.* Boston: Allyn and Bacon.

Rumbaut, R. (1989). The structure of refuge: Southeast Asian refugees in the United States, 1975–1985. *International Review of Comparative Public Policy, 1*, 97–129.

Skinner, K. (1980). Vietnamese in America: Diversity in adaptation. *California Sociologist, 3*, 103–124.

Solomon, B. B. (1985). Community social work practice in oppressed minority communities. In S. Taylor and R. Roberts (Eds.), *Theory and Practice of Community Social Work* (pp. 217–257). New York: Columbia University Press.

Taylor, R. (1979). Black ethnicity and the persistence of ethnogenesis. *American Journal of Sociology, 84*, 1401–1423.

Toennies, F. (1961). Gemeinschaft and gesellschaft. In T. Parsons, E. Shils, K. Naegele, and J. Potts (Eds.), *Theories of Society: Vol. 1.* (pp. 191–201). New York: Free Press.

Wacquant, L., and Wilson, W. (1993). The cost of racial and class exclusion in the inner city. In W. Wilson (Ed.), *The Ghetto Underclass.* Newbury Park, CA: Sage.

Warren, R. (1963). *The Community in America.* Chicago: Rand McNally.

Wilson, W. (1987). *The Truly Disadvantaged.* Chicago: University of Chicago Press.

Woldemikael, T. (1987). Assertion versus accomomodation: A comparative approach to intergroup relations. *American Behavioral Scientist, 30*, 411–428.

Zastrow, C. (1995). *The Practice of Social Work* (5th ed.). Pacific Grove, CA: Brooks/Cole.

Zippay, A. (1995). The politics of empowerment. *Social Work, 40*, 263–267.

6

Ethnicity and Social Services

The primary role of social services is to improve the functioning of the individual, family, group, or community. However, if problems are not perceived, the efforts of agencies to instill change are bound to fail. Social services can only be placed in a helping role if the need for help is recognized and the services themselves are perceived and accepted as helpers.

Social service agencies are primarily public agencies supported by federal, state, county, and municipal funds or private agencies funded by fees, United Way, contributions, grants, and donations. Private agencies are either sectarian (church- or religion-affiliated) or nonsectarian. However, most sectarian agencies are not restricted to services for their own group and serve others in the community. In fact, in many areas of the country, sectarian agencies such as Catholic Social Services or Jewish Family Services find that a majority of their clients are members of other religious groups. In addition, agencies may be mainstream in that they serve the entire community or ethnic group, focusing on only one population.

Mainstream Agencies

As society becomes increasingly diverse, mainstream agencies accustomed to serving the larger society are making serious attempts to serve ethnic populations effectively. In fact, ethnic-sensitive practice has become an aim of many programs. This type of practice is responsive and responsible to the culture of minority groups, understanding of an individual's personal values, and knowledgeable about and skillful in working with different cultures (Gutierrez, 1992).

To achieve this type of practice, agency administrators must be willing to examine their own ideologies and attitudes and the ways in which they affect the perception of problems and services. As an example, if truancy among African-American children is seen as reflecting a lack of parent involvement or teenage pregnancy as indicating a lack of knowledge of contraceptives, the interventions will focus on parenting skills and education. In addition, as these perceptions are based on agency ideology, workers will be expected to adhere to them in their assessments and case plans.

On the other hand, the agency using ethnic-sensitive practice will work toward examining the problems from the perspective of the clients. Understanding their values regarding truancy and education and teenage pregnancy and subsequent attitudes toward these concerns becomes a basis for further work. The perspective of the clients regarding these issues, and whether they are considered problems, is the framework for interventions. Ethnic-sensitive practice offers the means by which mainstream agencies can be responsive to diverse cultures.

However, ethnic-sensitive practice cannot in itself assure the use of services by ethnic groups. Groups' previous histories in dealing with services, particularly those that were government sponsored, affect the way such programs are perceived in this country. Those coming from oppressive and totalitarian regimes will be reluctant to seek help from publicly sponsored programs since, as suggested before, their previous experiences demanded invisibility from the government as the only way to maintain identity and security. Others, coming from traditions in which bribery and corruption were common among government agencies, are likely to mistrust public programs.

Ethnic Agencies

Ethnic agencies are those that concentrate on providing services to their own ethnic groups. Such agencies exist within many communities, including both well-established minority groups and those of new immigrants. The agencies engage in activities such as self-help, advocacy, education, counseling, and community development. Frequently the staff are local indigenous persons from the community, with the majority being paraprofessionals.

The most complete definition of an ethnic agency is provided by Jenkins (1981). The agency (1) serves primarily ethnic clients, (2) is staffed by a majority of individuals of the same ethnicity as the client group, (3) has an ethnic majority on the board, (4) has ethnic community or power structure support, (5) integrates ethnic content into its program, (6) views strengthening the family as a primary goal, and (7) maintains an ideology that promotes ethnic identity and ethnic participation in the decision-making process.

Deficiencies in the larger social system can also promote the formation of ethnic agencies (Inglehart and Becerra, 1995). These deficiencies include nonresponsiveness to community needs, intrusiveness of traditional agencies (which damages informal systems), a sense of powerlessness, paternalism, and myths and stereotypes regarding the community.

In addition to these deficiencies, barriers to utilization of traditional agencies can further influence the development of ethnic ones. Previous negative experiences with mainstream agencies, distrust, and unwillingness to share information with those outside of the community can foster the growth of local services. In fact, many may turn to these agencies primarily on the belief that they are more compatible with their own attitudes and experiences. With its close identification and links with the community, the ethnic agency is able to offer group members the support and understanding frequently lacking in mainstream social service agencies.

Given these factors, which can influence many to prefer ethnic services, it would appear that mainstream or traditional agencies would have little chance of competing effectively in ethnic communities. However, as the importance of ethnicity in persons' lives alters with other variables such as language and social class, ethnic agencies often have to compete with other services.

Middle-class ethnic members integrated into the society frequently prefer mainstream agencies, while lower class members remain more comfortable with the ethnic agency (Inglehart and Becerra, 1995). Poverty, combined with minority status, also creates a demand for ethnic-specific services, since persons feel that these programs are more closely connected with their needs.

Although the ethnic agency fills a significant gap in the provision of social services, it also has several shortcomings (Inglehart and Becerra, 1995). Among these are trying to do too much with too little (which can undermine effectiveness), blurring role boundaries with clients or making them ambiguous or blurred, and stereotyping the "out group." As agencies remain separated from the greater community, there is the risk of polarization of both services and clients. Both staff and those they serve are vulnerable to assuming that the greater society can never understand their concerns or adequately address their needs.

The group cohesiveness that underscores services and staff relationships with clients can work against agency effectiveness. Clients may in fact be reticent to share or disclose themselves if they feel the information is too deviant from cultural norms or may be leaked to others in the community. As an example, if mental problems are perceived as indicative of being cursed and are embarrassing to the family, clients are likely to be reticent in discussing them with ethnic members of their community, even though these members work for an agency.

Ethnic agencies, in their efforts to be accepted by the community, often stress their ethnicity over professionalism. Although this may increase their acceptance locally, it can also limit their links with mainstream social services. Agencies may be hesitant about making referrals to other agencies whose professionalism and credibility are in doubt. In addition, outsiders doubting the capability of the ethnic agency may be hesitant in allocating funds and resources to them. In addition, the absence of professionals can restrict the ability of the ethnic agency to compete successfully for grants for program development.

Ethnicity in Service Delivery

In her examination of ethnic social services, Jenkins (1981) identifies critical factors associated with the micro, mezzo, and macro levels of service delivery that determine the relative importance of ethnicity in services. The situation and its potential alternatives are viewed as most important at the micro, or case, level.

Depending upon the situation, someone of the same ethnic group may or may not be preferred to a professional from another group. As an example, the ethnicity of a dentist tends to have lower priority as a determining factor in utilization than the ethnicity of a social worker. In the latter situation, sharing a common background and ease of communication are necessary for involvement. These factors are less important in the selection of a dentist and, in fact, many persons may actually prefer an "American" dentist to one from their native country.

At the mezzo, or service delivery, level, characteristics of the group determine the relevance of ethnicity to service delivery. Length of time since immigration, degree of cultural assimilation, locale, class, and group homogeneity need to be considered. The perspectives and needs of second-generation immigrants regarding services will differ from those who have just arrived. Ethnic group members living in rural areas will likely have different perspectives regarding services than those in urban settings. For example, tribal affiliations and laws will be of less consequence for Indian families living in cities than for those living on reservations.

Social class is particularly important at the mezzo level, as it affects the preferences of both clients and workers. Middle-class persons tend to give exceptional credence to professional status and to prefer professionals over a member of the same ethnic group. These attitudes influence clients in their selection of agencies and workers in their relationships with other services.

The mezzo level of service delivery is also affected by the homogeneity of ethnic groups. As discussed earlier in the book, the Asian/Pacific Islander population and the Hispanic population are composed of many subgroups. The backgrounds and histories of these subgroups differ in many ways, which can impinge on their unity. Moreover, by assuming homogeneity based on common language and traditions, providers can overlook important differences, which can affect a willingness to use or interest in using services. At the same time, stressing differences among subgroups, rather than any similarities, can prevent any unity from occurring.

Finally, the macro level of service delivery is critical to ethnic services since it is this level that determines national policies affecting services. The ways in which countries perceive and treat immigrants, the status and acceptance of culturally diverse groups and their rights to services, and the extent to which homogeneity is sought are influential factors in the development of social policy. The impact of the macro level on policy and services has become particularly evident as concerns have been raised about the demands placed on society by new immigrants. Proposed legislation and efforts to restrict benefits to these persons underscores the impact that the macro level can have on social services.

Service Utilization

Availability

Services, regardless of the type of agency offering them, are used when they are available, accessible, and acceptable to the intended population (Wallace, 1990). Availability refers to the location and amount of services provided and whether they are sufficient to meet the groups' needs. A clinic located outside of an ethnic community, although on a bus line, may be perceived as unavailable if persons are uncomfortable leaving the boundaries of their particular neighborhood. Obviously, a limited amount of services, such as English classes, can seriously curtail service availability.

Accessibility

Accessibility depends upon persons' knowledge of programs and having the necessary resources, such as finances, insurance, or transportation, needed for utilization. Accessibility is also affected by the degree of coordination or fragmentation among services. Referring persons to other departments or programs, often located in a different locality, can be detrimental to service use. Navigating between services is often particularly difficult for ethnic group members who are less familiar with the larger community and uncomfortable in seeking help outside of their own neighborhood.

Accessibility also depends upon service providers' ability to reach those in need. Language can be a major barrier to accessibility. Making sure that the person who answers the agency telephone is fluent in the language of the residents is of prime importance, since he or she is often the first contact that the potential client has with the agency. Having workers who speak the same dialects as the residents and assuring that their accents are compatible with the group are important factors in accessibility.

For example, the heterogeneity among the Hispanic population can affect service use, as accents and even vocabulary often differ. Cuban families may find it difficult to understand Puerto Rican workers and, in some instances, may even be reluctant to use services in which they are involved. Having brochures and other material about the services in the native language can greatly increase access, but, at the same time, these materials should also be designed so that they can be understood by persons whose reading skills, even within their own language, can be very limited.

Within ethnic minority communities with high crime rates, access is often impeded by worker concerns about safety. As an example, offering Acquired Immunodeficiency Syndrome (AIDS) care to homebound patients in many urban areas is frequently very difficult because nurses feel uneasy about entering the community. In these instances, additional security measures, such as using two workers, are often required to help facilitate access.

Service accessibility is also dependent upon the effectiveness of the outreach activities. Outreach involves actively informing the community about the service and its goals and making them attractive to the residents. Outreach workers are active in the community describing their services and making them attractive to potential clients. Rather than waiting for persons to come to the agencies, they attend local functions, give talks at community organizations, and meet with people in the neighborhoods. The aim is to encourage service use by demonstrating the accessibility of the program.

Involving local leaders such as the clergy, media personalities, and teachers can be important in the success of the outreach activity.

Finally, even the titles of agencies can affect accessibility. Within ethnic communities mental problems are often a source of shame and mental health counseling is not trusted. Consequently, calling a service "Center for Mental Health" is likely to deter access. Instead, a title which emphasizes growth or acceptable concerns such as "healthy living" may encourage persons to seek further information regarding services.

Many factors can improve accessibility. Locating services in ethnic areas and providing free transportation and information about the services in the local mass media and in the native language are effective means of increasing access. In addition, having providers, including those who answer the telephone, speak in the native language can be a critical factor in service utilization.

Acceptability

In order for services to be used, they must be acceptable to the ethnic group. Cultural values and traditions as they affect attitudes and behavior are major influences in acceptability. For example, services such as day care, family planning, and mental health counseling may strongly conflict with traditional values. However, as persons become assimilated into the greater society and its values, these traditional values are often modified. Thus, as women become employed and seek more independence, using day care services for their children and family planning for themselves tends to become more acceptable.

Seeking formal assistance may be perceived as representing a lack of pride, with those using services stigmatized. Admitting a need for help or showing a willingness to discuss problems with strangers can be culturally unacceptable. In fact, some research (Cox and Monk, 1990) has shown that, rather than reducing stress, the receipt of services such as home care may actually aggravate it. In this instance the receipt of home help assistance to care for an elderly relative with dementia, rather than ameliorating stress among Hispanic caregivers, actually increased it, as the use of the service was in conflict with traditional norms of family support.

Service acceptability is also affected by the use of indigenous personnel. These persons can assist in bridging the gap between services and clients because they share a common historical, cultural, and linguistic background with the client population. They increase rapport and communication between providers and potential ethnic clients through their insights and information (Brawley and Schindler, 1991). As these persons are able to interact easily with the community, they are important representatives of the service and have major roles in interpreting its programs and goals.

As well as having staff from the local community, having administrative boards composed of local persons also contributes to acceptability. The board members act as links with the community, spokespersons for the service agency, and important informants regarding the traditions and needs of those the agency is trying to serve.

The administrative structure and procedures of the agency are also important in acceptability. For example, persons may be deterred from using services if they are expected to be interviewed by several persons. This type of procedure, acceptable to others in society, can be unacceptable to those accustomed to informal and close relationships. Information necessary to determine eligibility is perceived as too intrusive and confidential and this acts as a barrier to service acceptability. Many ethnic groups perceive demands for papers, referrals, and forms as intrusive and indicative of callous providers.

Assuring that cultural preferences of the population are met assists in program acceptance. A nutrition program for Hispanic elderly that serves hamburgers and hot dogs is less likely to be attended than one that serves traditional Hispanic foods. In many cultures, services will not be used if the providers are of the opposite sex or if they are perceived as being too young. For example, Portuguese men are unlikely to discuss their marital problems with female social workers, and elderly Cambodians feel uneasy sharing their concerns with counselors who are the same ages as their children.

The experiences of groups with services in their own countries can also affect their acceptance of services. Those coming from countries where the government controlled most aspects of their lives perceive social agencies as instruments of social control. Rather than turning to agencies for assistance, such persons tend to avoid them. If compelled to use agencies or social workers, they are apt to feel threatened. As an example, Russian parents may be hostile to school social workers, who are perceived as threatening to their children and family. Understanding the reasons for their attitudes and behaviors is essential in order for the service to be reinterpreted and made acceptable to the family.

Predisposing, Enabling, and Need Factors in Utilization

The model of health care behavior developed by Andersen and Newman (1973) has frequently been used as a framework for understanding the use of social services. The model conceives of utilization as resulting from three groups of factors: predisposing, enabling, and need. Predisposing factors are demographic characteristics such as age, marital status, education, and attitudes toward services. Enabling factors include economic resources such as income and insurance and social resources such as transportation and assistance. The need variables, which are frequently most important in the decision, include physical health, mental health, and functional status.

In work with ethnic groups, each of these categories can act as particularly salient determinants of service utilization. Comparable to the factors affecting acceptability discussed earlier, attitudes toward services, whether or not they are perceived as meaningful and appropriate, are strongly influenced by ethnic values and experiences. Cultural values that stress informal care or privacy can act as major barriers to the use of formal services. For example, a study of hospital discharge planning found that African-American families maintained strong negative feelings toward nursing homes and that these feelings were important factors in their discharge plans (Cox and Verdeick, 1994).

However, it is important not to attribute negative attitudes solely to cultural values. These predisposing attitudes may also be affected by previous negative experiences with services. Poor care, long waits in uncomfortable waiting rooms, and insensitive providers are among the many factors affecting the predisposition of persons toward the use of services. Thus, a preference for informal care and an aversion to nursing homes is as likely to reflect a history of deteriorating wards and poorly trained staff as it is specific values.

The previous experiences with services in their native countries often affect the attitudes and even the behaviors of immigrants toward services in the United States. As an example, Soviet émigrés are unaccustomed to voluntary services, as all services in the Soviet Union are public. Employees of these services are frequently manipulated by clients as a means to receiving better care (Drachman and Halberstadt, 1992). These attitudes and behaviors are transferred to interactions with service providers in the United States, and can cause resentment among workers, who perceive these émigrés as demanding and aggressive.

In working with ethnic communities and individuals, close attention must also be given to the enabling factors, those which facilitate service utilization. Primary among these factors are insurance coverage, income, and often eligibility for benefits such as Medicaid or for services. In addition, using indigenous personnel who are familiar with the culture and attitudes of the population can be important enabling factors, for they can interpret the services to the community, as well as educate other providers about traditional help-seeking behaviors of the group.

Immigration status and concerns can also act as a major enabling factor affecting the use of services. Fears associated with rights and documentation often lead to hesitancy regarding eligibility and even fears that service use may result in deportation. These fears are heightened if there is a history of agencies reporting undocumented persons to authorities. All the same, new immigrants are often in dire need of services due to financial problems, intergenerational conflicts, and stresses associated with attempting to adapt to the new society. Adjusting to the new country requires knowledge and support, but fear of deportation can prevent many from using needed services, placing them at grave risk when economic, health, housing, and family needs are not met (Drachman, 1995).

Need factors are frequently the most influential in determining the use of services. Individuals and groups use services when they perceive a need for assistance that can be met by the agency. However, the perception of need is strongly affected by cultural values and expectations. Thus, if aggression is considered normal for children and confusion is considered a normal behavior for the elderly, families are unlikely to perceive them as problems requiring assistance. In the same manner, years of discrimination can affect the expectations and perceived needs of a group or community. Having become accustomed to discrimination and few opportunities for advancement, community persons are unlikely to feel a strong interest in programs that promise job training and future economic success.

The link that persons make between their needs and available services is critical for utilization. In order for persons to use mental health counseling, they must perceive that they have a problem that counseling can solve. Before groups will participate in job training programs, they have to identify their problems as resulting from lack of skills and view the programs as potentially effective in improving their position.

Agency Staff

Staff reflect the agency, its relationships with the community, and its relationships with the greater society. Regardless of the type of agency or its auspices, it is the direct interactions of staff with clients that personify the agency. These interactions are the framework for all service delivery to individuals, groups, or communities.

Ethnic Staff

Staff from the same ethnic background as the clients often have an easier time establishing rapport with community members than do those from outside the ethnic group. Persons are less likely to feel that they have to explain or justify themselves to workers from the same background who share the same history and experiences. Language barriers are also reduced, which enables practitioners to obtain a clear understanding of the problem and to more easily discuss with the client possible interventions. It is important to note that, although this similarity can be important in developing immediate rapport, it does not necessarily lead to greater trust or more effective functioning.

Clients are often suspicious of ethnic group members returning to a neighborhood as agency staff. Because staff have left the traditional community, persons frequently find it difficult to trust them or their motives. As an example, urbanized Native Americans may find it difficult to develop relationships with those living on reservations who question their tribal allegiance. Consequently, such Native American social workers have to make special efforts to overcome these suspicions and assure that the services are attractive to potential clients and groups. Ethnic group membership in itself is not sufficient.

As noted earlier in this chapter, as persons become more assimilated to society, particularly as they join the middle class, they frequently prefer workers from the majority population. Staff of their own ethnicity may be perceived as less qualified and less competent. In these situations, clients who are compelled to see an ethnic worker are liable to resist the relationship. In fact, the possibilities for misperception in these situations are great. The agency is likely to believe that by providing ethnic clients with an ethnic worker, they are sensitively attempting to meet their clients' concerns. However, the clients may perceive that, by being assigned this worker, they are being stereotyped and are being denied workers of equal worth.

Cultural Competence

It is obviously impossible for workers to pretend to possess ethnic identities that are not their own. In general, minorities respond badly and with hurt feelings to outsiders who pretend to be insiders. Jews traditionally interpret "some of my best friends are Jews" as an indicator of anti-Semitism. African Americans generally interpret as racist attempts by others to espouse their sensitivity and committment to African-American causes and view with suspicion workers who attempt to use African-American slang or phrases in their conversations.

Inappropriate equating of one's own experiences with that of an ethnic American is another example of cross-cultural incompetence. As an example, anecdotes of foreign travel experiences, by indicating the worker's wealth and status, can increase rather than decrease his or her distance from the client. Such stories may only serve to emphasize the difference in wealth and resources between the worker and the client.

A culturally competent professional approach, rather, is based on knowledge of other cultures and empathy for those who have suffered in the past. Immigrants and members of minority groups are affected by stressors that are often invisible to members of the majority culture. Working with others who are different demands both understanding of their cultural norms and perceptiveness about the ways in which traditional ethnic patterns are threatened by the intra- and intergenerational processes of acculturation.

For example, if family relationships and children's respect for parental authority are salient values within a specific group, adolescents' demands for autonomy can pose formidable challenges for less assimilated parents. A knowledge of the traditional norms and expectations and how the adolescent is threatening them is basic to cultural competence. In the same way, the culturally competent worker will recognize that, in contrast to most other clients, many Asian families will expect to bring an older family member to an appointment to share in the discussion of child-rearing issues and parenting.

Though basic cultural knowledge is essential, it is only through working with clients, whether individuals, groups, or communities, that the practitioner is able to achieve genuine understanding of the impact of certain attitudes and behaviors on the traditional system. Moreover, it is only through work with ethnic groups that one becomes aware of the impact that the structure and organization of the agency can have on these clients. For example, agencies that reduce or do not charge fees for services may be shunned by groups who feel stigmatized and devalued by charity. Regardless of their need for assistance, clients are likely to avoid these programs.

Evaluation

Evaluation of social services is becoming increasingly important, because agencies are responsible for demonstrating their effectiveness in order to receive funding. Generally, there are two methods of evaluation. Pract evaluation examines whether interventions are helping clients to reach their intended goals. Program evaluation determines whether the programs and services are reaching their objectives.

Most evaluation models consist of measures of inputs, interventions, outputs, and outcome variables. In working with ethnic groups, the following input factors are needed: cultural knowledge and skill in understanding and addressing the client's needs, ability to communicate, accurate perception of the client, problem identification, and appropriate resources to address the problems. Input factors at the program level include the ethnic backgrounds of the staff, cultural training and education, outreach to the community, composition of the board membership, community links, and program activities.

Culturally appropriate interventions are sensitive to values and norms governing behavior, as well as to the unique experiences of the client. At the individual level, evaluation of the interventions usually measures the extent to which a client has met a specific goal, with goal attainment scales often used to measure change and progress. As helpful as these instruments may be, they can be threatening to ethnic clients, who view counseling as an informal helping process. Formalizing and even quantifying the counseling relationship through the use of a scale could actually have a destructive effect on the relationship. With many clients or groups, it may be better simply to ask them to rate the progress they feel they have made toward each goal.

At the program level, interventions include the assessment process, type of counseling, referral procedures, and services. These interventions must be able to engage the individual client or group effectively. Program evaluation at this level is often done by collecting data on the number of cases opened, the types of problems presented, the services offered, and the referrals to and from the agency. Collecting this data on ethnic groups indicates the extent of their involvement with the agency and the areas in which more interaction may be necessary.

For the individual client, output is the immediate result of the intervention. Returning to school or becoming employed are examples of immediate output measures. Examples of output indicators at the program level are the initiation of new services or the implementation of a new policy. English classes for new immigrants or policies that recognize the special health care needs of elderly native Americans are programmatic output measures that indicate a service's responsiveness to ethnic group needs.

The outcome is the long-range benefit to the client, such as increased self-esteem or financial security. For a group or community, the desired

improvement in status and greater mobility within soci-
riables are particularly important at the program level as
justify the program's very existence. If an agency can
t, as a result of its work, ethnic group members are less de-
lic support and better able to compete in society, it will be
ition to warrant further funding. However, such justification is often very difficult, depending as it does on being able to prove that the desired outcomes are linked to the specific service inputs.

Knowledge for Service Delivery

Agency staff, whether or not they are members of the ethnic group, must be sensitive to their own beliefs, stereotypes, and prejudices. Without this knowledge, clients and their problems are unlikely to be accurately perceived, since they will be distorted by practitioners' own perspectives.

As an example, if practitioners, through their own stereotypes, perceive an ethnic group as not having any interest in education, parents' lack of involvement in schools will be seen as evidence in support of this trait. Subsequent efforts to stimulate involvement that do not target the underlying reasons for the lack of interest are bound to fail. On the other hand, by learning the reasons for the lack of parental involvement, such as parents' previous experiences with the school system and efforts to change it, practitioners will be better able to develop appropriate interventions, which can encourage parental involvement.

As indicated throughout the chapter, practitioners must be knowledgeable about group culture and traditions in order to establish relationships. This knowledge is conveyed to the client by recognizing the stresses and conflicts that may be related to the decision to seek services. Showing families an awareness of the ambivalence they may have felt in discussing their problems associated with the care of an elderly parent, or demonstrating to community leaders that you realize their concerns about involving an outsider in their neighborhood plans, reflects understanding of traditions and values necessary for mutuality in the helping relationship.

Knowledge about the potential obstacles to change is critical, as it can assist in the formation of realistic expectations and goals. As an example, clients may be opposed to counseling for children but willing to discuss child-rearing practices or discipline measures. Groups may be unwilling to discuss spousal abuse but will share views regarding women's roles and needs. Knowing how values affect the lives of ethnic groups and their objectives for change provides a framework for the evolving relationship.

Being knowledgeable about the history of the ethnic group and the factors contributing to emigration can be particularly significant for understanding present perspectives and concerns. The histories of refugees are often replete with stories of violence, war, and slaughter, and always involve the uprooting and separation of families. The trauma of leaving a homeland and adjusting to a new society has strong implications for individual well-being. In addition, the role of social agencies in the native country will influence the way in which such agencies are perceived. By understanding the group's history, any misconceptions regarding the agency and the role of the worker that could pose obstacles to service can be addressed.

In developing relationships, practitioners must be careful not to use global knowledge in making generalizations about groups or clients. Often there is a temptation to proceed from the general cultural information to the specific client, a process that will be unfounded when the information does not necessarily apply to the person in the office (Sue,1988; Sue and Zane,1987). For example, assuming that a Mexican-American woman is opposed to contraception or that a group of Korean children is most concerned with academic achievement may be inaccurate. Indeed, the woman may be eager to discuss birth control and the children may be most interested in joining a soccer club. In this instance, the global knowledge obscures the specific needs and interests and actually undermines relationships.

Focusing on the cultural background can also blur the uniqueness of the individual client and the factors important in his or her life. Being dominated by a cultural perspective can cause practitioners to overlook critical factors more closely related to the presenting problem (Gelfand and Fandetti, 1986). The reluctance of an elderly Russian woman to attend a senior center could be due to a lack of transportation rather than a cultural norm that says the elderly should remain at home. Reluctance of a Cambodian woman to attend parenting classes is as likely to be due to having no one with whom to leave her child as it is to resistance to learning new skills. These factors, which strongly affect the presenting problems, can be obscured by the opaque ethnic lens.

Agencies and staff must also recognize the realities of the environment and the social conditions of the group. The types of discrimination encountered and the value that society places on the ethnic group cannot be ignored in attempting to understand present functioning and responses to social programs. Realizing that behaviors and problems are frequently the outcomes of social stresses rather than individual pathology is critical in work with ethnic populations. For example, the African-American mother who will not allow her 3-year-old outside to play is likely to be reacting to the reality of violence in the neighborhood, rather than manifesting overprotective behavior or poor mothering skills.

Services and the Ethnic Lens

Designing social services that are effective in reaching and serving ethnic groups is a major challenge to the profession. The ethnic lens, as it affects clients' perception of services and practitioners' perceptions of clients and their needs, plays a pivotal role in social work's ability to meet this challenge. Consequently, it is incumbent upon agencies to assure that these lenses are free from distortion.

One of the first issues ethnic groups are likely to confront in their perception of the agency is whether the agency is fundamentally "ours" or "theirs," whether it is one that welcomes "people like us" or has staff "like us." Often, this question is not resolvable simply by official policy or statement, because past experiences have frequently taught many ethnic groups that such statements are not reliable. Informal comments, community gossip, rumors, and personal references from former clients can count for much more than stated policies.

As an example, rumors that a program is racist or is supported by funds from white supremacists can deter potential African-American clients regardless of the program's actual intent and policy. In this instance, previous experiences increase the credibility of these rumors and influence the groups' perception of the program.

Staff persons who are "like us" can make communication easier, due to the histories they share with prospective clients. The terms used to describe the discovery of an Italian-American or African-American staff member are themselves powerful. Reports of a "paisan" or a "brother" among the staff can affect the entire ethnic lens. The agency is transformed into a place that is both welcoming and accommodating to "us."

A complicating phenomenon, self-hatred (Lewin, 1948; Pinderhughes, 1989), can also modify and distort the lens. This occurs when ethnic group members internalize the negative stereotypic views of others. "Good" becomes the way the majority look, act, think, and live. The way "we" behave is devalued and less than acceptable. Physical features, languages, and a wide range of other phenomena lend themselves to becoming vehicles for self-hatred. Self-hatred is an insidious phenomenon, widespread and yet often denied, because it is viewed as dishonorable. It is an indicator that people accept their differences as "inferior" and that they do not conform in many important ways to the expectations of others.

Self-hatred can influence how agencies are viewed in several ways. One of the clearest has to do with sponsorship, auspices, and even the name of the organization. Names such as African-American Men's Cultural Center, Jewish Family Service, or Aurelia Gomez Outpatient Clinic may be perceived as places where one will be understood and accepted or, conversely, as places that evoke shame and doubt. If the latter is true, such persons are likely to seek care from an "American" agency.

Few people are without some conflict about the group to which they belong. Immigrants may seek, often with ambivalence, a "real American" place because of a devaluing of their cultural traditions and their concern about being accepted into the greater society. Thus, these internal concerns modify their own ethnic lens.

Schwartz (1961, 1976) saw one of the core functions of the social worker as searching out the common ground. He was addressing work with groups, but we would suggest that the same concept applies to working with individuals, families, and communities. Without giving up one's professional identity, values, and goals, and without asking clients and client-systems to give up their ethnic lenses, the task becomes one of helping to search out and identify the common ground. This includes the problem definitions, help, processes, and time frames on which both the worker and the client can agree.

A commonly shared characteristic of ethnic groups is a greater degree of trust in personal relationships and communication than in official and bureaucratic procedures. The implications for the behavior of social workers, program planners, and administrators are clear and direct.

First, one should not pose as an expert on another's culture or community. Respect for ethnic diversity requires a stance that emphasizes listening. Every ethnic group has its own stories of outsiders, often official people who thought they knew better but who, in fact, made it clear that they knew little or nothing.

Second, those working with clients or communities of a particular ethnic identity need to establish credibility. This can be accomplished in several ways but each requires consciousness and sensitivity in order to learn the important concepts of the group. In terms of our model, this can be thought of as spending time learning how things look through the ethnic lens of the group.

Third, decisions, programs, and interventions imposed on individuals or groups by outside authorities are likely to be viewed with suspicion and hostility. Participation by group members and leaders and careful communication with the community of potential clients and consumers is essential.

Finally, it is imperative to recognize that all cultural patterns are based on a universal human need: to solve problems of human existence and find meaning in the face of physical, social, and technological ecologies. The framework for social work involvement must respect and legitimize the diverse ways in which ethnicity can influence the efforts to solve these problems. By working through a clear ethnic lens that recognizes the factors that can impede growth and functioning, while also recognizing cultural strengths and preferences, social services can enable ethnic persons and groups to obtain the benefits ascribed to others in society.

Questions for Discussion

1. Discuss what is meant by ethnic-sensitive practice and how it may be incorporated into a social service agency.
2. What factors may affect persons' willingness to use an ethnic agency?
3. Describe the roles of availability, accessibility, and acceptability in service utilization by ethnic group members and give examples of ways to assure their presence.
4. What is meant by cultural competence?
5. How might "self-hatred" affect service delivery to ethnic clients?

References

Andersen, R., and Newman, J. (1973). Societal and individual determinants of medical care utilization in the United States. *Milbank Memorial Fund Quarterly, 51*, 95–124.

Brager, G. (1965). The indigenous worker: A new approach to the social work technician. *Social Work, 10*, 124–130.

Brawley, E., and Schindler, R. (1991). Strengthening professonal and paraprofessional contributions to social service and social development. *British Journal of Social Work, 21*, 515–531.

Cox, C., and Monk, A. (1990). Minority caregivers of dementia victims: A comparison of Black and Hispanic families. *Journal of Applied Gerontology, 9*, 340–355.

Cox, C., and Verdeick, M. (1994). Factors affecting the outcomes of hospitalized dementia patients: From home to hospital to discharge. *Gerontologist, 34,* 497–504.

Drachman, D. (1995). Immigration statuses and their influence on service provision, access, and use. *Social Work, 40,* 188–197.

Drachman, D., and Halberstadt, A. (1992). A stage of migration framework as applied to recent soviet emigres. *Journal of Multicultural Social Work, 2,* 63–75.

Gelfand, D., and Bialik-Gilad, R. (1989). Immigration reform and social work. *Social Work, 34,* 23–27.

Gelfand, D., and Fandetti, D. (1986). The emergent nature of ethnicity: Dilemmas in assessment. *Social Casework, 67,* 542–550.

Glasser, I. (1983). Guidelines for using an interpreter in social work. *Child Welfare, 57,* 468–470.

Green, J. (1995). *Cultural Awareness in the Human Services: A Multi-Ethnic Approach* (2nd ed.). Boston: Allyn and Bacon.

Gutierrez, L. (1992). Empowering ethnic minorities in the twenty-first century. In Y. Hasenfeld (Ed.), *Human Services as Complex Organizations* (pp. 320–338). Newbury Park, CA: Sage.

Hurdle, D. (1991). *The Ethnic Group Experience.* New York: Springer.

Inglehart, A., and Becerra, R. (1995). *Social Services and the Ethnic Community.* Boston: Allyn and Bacon.

Jenkins, S. (1981). *The Ethnic Dilemma in Social Services.* New York: Free Press.

Kamikawa, L. (1987). *Health Care: The Pacific/Asian Perspective* (Monograph). Seattle, WA: National Pacific/Asian Resource Center.

Lewin, K. (1948). *Resolving Social Conflicts.* New York: Harper & Row.

Pinderhughes, E. (1989). *Understanding, Race, Ethnicity, and Power.* New York: Free Press.

Schwartz, W. (1961). *New Perspectives on Services to Groups: Social Work with Groups.* Silver Spring, MD: National Association of Social Workers.

Schwartz, W. (1976). Between client and system: The mediating function. In R. Roberts and H. Northen (Eds.), *Theories of Social Work with Groups* (pp. 171–197). New York: Columbia University Press.

Sue, S. (1988). Psychotherapeutic services to ethnic minorities: Two decades of research findings. *American Psychologist, 43,* 301–308.

Sue, S., and Sue, D. (1977). Barriers to effective cross-cultural counseling. *Journal of Counseling Psychology, 24,* 420–429.

Sue, S., and Zane, N. (1987). The role of culture and cultural techniques in psychotherapy. *American Psychologist, 42,* 37–45.

Wallace, S. (1990). The no-care zone: Availability, accessibility, acceptability in community based long term care. *Gerontologist, 30,* 254–261.

7

Ethnicity and Health

Health and health care are complex issues, which have recently warranted much attention in the United States. Policy reform, the cost of health care, the use of health services, the spread of diseases such as AIDS, and the chronic illnesses and care required by the elderly are among the major issues confronting policy makers and administrators. The complexity of dealing with each of these areas is compounded by ethnicity inasmuch as minority individuals are most likely to be in poverty and dependent upon publicly supported health programs while their risks for many chronic illnesses remain high.

Because they are involved in social policy planning, health care research, administration, and direct services to patients and their families, social workers play active roles in the health care field. Moreover, as culture can affect the perception and even the experience of illness and its care, as well as the propensity toward prevention, social work can have a vital place in improving the health status and situations of these diverse populations.

Data from *Healthy People 2000* (U.S. Department of Health and Human Services [DHHS], 1992) document the disparities in health existing among minority groups. The largest minority group, African Americans, shows a large disparity in rates of chronic illnesses and causes of death from those of non-whites. The risk of cancer is higher among African-American men, and the chances of five-year survival are significantly less. Diabetes is 33% more common among blacks than whites and is highest among black women, whose risks for complications are also higher. Black babies are twice as likely as white babies to die before their first birthday, with low birth weights accounting for many of these deaths. Homicide is the most frequent cause of death for young African-American men and is seven times more prevalent than among whites. Contributing to these conditions are the risk factors of poor nutrition, smoking, alcohol and drug abuse, lack of routine preventive health care, and greater propensity to use emergency rooms and clinics and to have no usual source of medical care.

The health of the Hispanic population varies among its many subgroups. Mexican Americans have low rates of cardiovascular disease, while among Puerto Ricans in New York the rate of stroke is very high. Cuban Americans have high utilization rates of prenatal care, but low rates exist among Mexican Americans and Puerto Ricans. Smoking, use of alcohol, and drug abuse remain higher among Hispanic populations while preventive care is less frequent than among non-Hispanic whites.

As noted in the DHHS report, it is difficult to adequately describe the health of Asian and Pacific Islander Americans, due to the many subgroups and immigration experiences of this population. The health status and diseases afflicting such persons born in the United States does not differ from those of white Americans. Conversely, recent immigrants from Southeast Asia have high rates of tuberculosis and hepatitis B. The rate of smoking among immigrants is also extremely high, ranging from 65% for Vietnamese to 92% for Laotians, as compared with 30% for the overall American population.

Injuries, cirrhosis, homicide, suicide, pneumonia, and complications of diabetes account for excessive deaths among American Indian and Alaskan Native populations, which would not have occurred if the death rates were comparable to those of the total population. In early adulthood, the death rate of these groups is twice that of the U.S. population as a whole. Alcohol is a major factor in these excessive deaths, as it contributes to injuries associated with automobile accidents, homicides, and suicide. Cirrhosis and diabetes are the two most frequently reported chronic diseases among these populations.

These data strikingly demonstrate the relationship of ethnicity and culture to health and health status. Smoking, use of alcohol and drugs, bad nutrition, and lack of exercise are risk factors that have been closely identified with heart disease, cancer, AIDS, and liver disease, but the extent to which individual behaviors are shaped and moderated by these risks will to a large extent depend upon perceptions and sociocultural processes and norms. Altering these behaviors will be dependent upon the degree to which groups accept the reality of the risks they present, as well as their willingness to change.

Factors Affecting the Use of Services

The utilization of health services by ethnic minority groups will depend in large part upon their availability, accessibility, and acceptability. Services must be located within ethnic communities or within reach by use of public transportation. If services are not available, persons are more likely to delay treatment until conditions become grave enough that they interfere with their usual activities. By the time treatment is received, conditions may be advanced and demand much more aggressive care. Consequently, delays place greater burdens on both the individual and the medical care system. But, as many urban and rural areas lack sufficient public health clinics or depend on free voluntary clinics, where waits may be very long, availability remains a barrier to care.

A major factor in accessibility is income and insurance. Ethnic minority persons are among those most likely to be in poverty and thus without private insurance. As an example, a 1985 study of minorities in Boston found that 12% of whites lacked health insurance, in comparison with 19% of blacks, 27% of Hispanics, and 27% of Asian Pacific Islanders (Gold and Socolar, 1987). Moreover, a large proportion of those uninsured were employed but had low incomes and employers who did not provide insurance. Lacking the means to afford medical care, they tended to delay use of services.

Fragmentation of the health care system can act as another barrier to utilization for ethnic groups. This fragmentation, which is often the result of different funding sources and various service providers, affects access because it requires individuals frequently to navigate a maze of papers, forms, and facilities. The tendency toward specialization, which is common in medical practice, can further deter utilization by those who seek a holistic mode of treatment.

The degree of access will depend upon the individual's ability and motivation to follow through on referrals and procedures, as well as his or her language and understanding of the system's demands. For many ethnic group members, this process is difficult and is perceived as a symbol of the insensitivity and lack of caring of the health care providers.

Accessibility may also by affected by the legal status of the ethnic groups. Illegal immigrants, worried about deportation, will be anxious about using services that demand the completion of many forms and papers. Persons who are waiting for legal residency may be afraid to use services due to fears that utilization could jeopardize their status. In addition, recent attention to the issues associated with undocumented aliens and their use of services can further deter many from applying for Medicaid benefits or using public services.

Acceptability of medical care by ethnic groups is associated with the degree to which the services meet cultural values, norms, and expectations. Having providers of the same ethnic group, who speak the same language, and are familiar with the culture and its traditions and values are factors that can increase acceptability. Providers who perceive the patients through an ethnic lens that is unbiased, knowledgeable, and respectful are likely to increase service acceptability by ethnic groups.

Ethnicity, Health, and Illness

Illness and health appear to be objective states, but much research has found that they are closely associated with ethnicity and cultural experiences. Thus, even the perception of pain and suffering has been found to be influenced by ethnicity. In an early study on the relationship of pain to culture, Zborowski (1952) observed that Jewish, Italian, and "Old Stock" American patients responded to pain in distinct ways. Italian and Jewish patients tended to exaggerate the pain, with the latter also extremely concerned with the significance of the pain and what it might represent. In contrast, the "Old Stock" group tended to be stoic and to show much less concern about the discomfort.

Given that ethnicity can influence the perception of pain, it is not surprising that illness itself is also viewed through an ethnic lens. The identification of health and well-being and illness and incapacity are strongly influenced by cultural beliefs and values. Thus, if particular symptoms or disabilities are accepted as normal consequences of life, they are unlikely to be perceived as illnesses for which one seeks medical care. These perceptions affect the entire life course, from the very young to the very old. As an example, if diarrhea and consistent crying are considered to be normal patterns for newborn infants, parents are unlikely to seek medical care. If confusion and memory loss are expected behaviors among the elderly, adult children are less likely to perceive them as problems requiring assistance.

The reasons for seeking medical care and the problems for which treatments are sought are also influenced by ethnicity. In an early study of the relationship of ethnicity to the decision to seek medical care, Zola (1973) found that Italians sought care for symptoms that interfered with their relations or when an interpersonal crisis called attention to them. In contrast, Irish and Anglo-Saxon patients were more likely to seek medical attention when the symptoms threatened to interfere with their physical functioning or work.

Zborowski's study of how culture affects even the response to pain found Italian Americans to be concerned mainly with the immediacy of the pain, while Jewish Americans were concerned with the meaning of the pain and its affect on health and welfare. "Old Stock" Americans also focused on the significance of the pain but were generally more optimistic than the Jewish patients.

Cox (1986), in a comparison of the use of physicians among Vietnamese, Portuguese, and Hispanic elderly, found varying factors contributing to each group's decision to seek physician care. Among the Portuguese, being married contributed to physician care, while among the Hispanics being unmarried was a determinant of care. Although the three groups had similar prevalence rates of hypertension, it was a predictor of care only for the Vietnamese. Conversely, having a poor health status was related to physician use by the Portuguese and the Hispanics, but not by the Vietnamese, who rated their health the poorest.

Understanding cultural definitions of illness and the problems that influence the use of medical treatment is a prerequisite for effective health care. Social workers, in their interactions with patients, physicians, and other health care providers, have strategic roles as they help to clarify the ethnic lens of each group. Ensuring that providers are educated and knowledgeable about cultural beliefs and behaviors that can affect care and that patients understand and are amenable to varying modes of treatment and settings are major health care tasks.

Ethnicity can be a major influence on the ways in which persons respond to illness, or their "illness behavior." Staying in bed, ignoring the illness, or consuming chicken soup are examples of behaviors influenced by cultural traditions and belief systems. But it is important to also note that such behaviors do not necessarily negate the use of medical care. In fact, it is not uncommon for persons to integrate their traditional practices into modern medical care. As an example, using acupuncture or taking special herbal teas while under a physician's care is not unusual.

Mechanic (1978) identifies several factors that should be considered by health workers in their efforts to work with diverse cultural groups. If family and companionship are central values, the hospital is likely to be perceived as threatening. The hospital's isolation of the sick individual with accompanying restrictions can cause a greater sense of "aloneness." This can be alien to the need for companionship and familial interaction. Groups that are oriented toward the present rather than the future are often reluctant to undergo pain and discomfort, including inoculations for protection against future disease.

Diets and beliefs about foods may be associated with social or religious practices and are therefore difficult to change. Certain foods may be unacceptable, while others may have to be prepared in particular ways. Effecting changes in these practices can be difficult if they are not introduced in a culturally acceptable way. In addition, to the extent that healing is perceived as an art, rather than a scientific practice, people are likely to remain skeptical of modern medical practice and procedures. At the same time, as persons are assimilated into the greater society and health care is accessible, it is not uncommon for them to utilize both systems of care.

Integrating folk healing and modern medical treatment without perceiving the two as being in conflict is possible (Applewhite, 1995). Elderly Mexican Americans are able to accept each method according to which is most accessible and appropriate to the problem. Thus, Applewhite found that persons tended to rely on modern health care for major problems and herbal remedies for minor ailments, with many using both systems of care simultaneously.

Understanding folk beliefs is critical to the effectiveness of health care. As an example, spiritism and folk healers are important components of Puerto Rican culture and, in order to reach many individuals, their roles must be understood (Delgado, 1988). Puerto Rican folk healing consists of herbal medicine and "satiguando," a folk healer who treats intestinal disorders, muscle aches, and broken bones. In addition, Puerto Rican spiritism is based on the belief that the visible world is surrounded by an invisible world inhabited by good and evil spirits who influence behaviors and many problems. To remedy these ills, individuals often go to mediums or spiritists who practice healing. If the illness is the will of God, either as a test or as a punishment, the medium will not be able to help, but if it is due to any other reason, help is expected.

In engaging and treating Puerto Rican clients, Delgado suggests that social workers adopt some of the group methods and principles of spiritism. Consequently, using groups and themes that involve interpersonal and environmental issues are likely to attract these clients. Incorporating many aspects of spiritism such as activities, involvement of the members, and active participation of the leader is a strategy that can increase the acceptance of therapy and treatment, because they are being made culturally acceptable.

Understanding unique cultural ways of treatment is important not only as a means of reaching ethnic clients but also to assure that such treatments are not misinterpreted. As an example, Vietnamese often rub their children with coins as a means of treating fevers and other ailments. Without a knowledge of the Vietnamese culture, health care professionals can mistake the marks left by this rubbing as evidence of child abuse. Refusing to take an elderly parent suffering from chronic pain to a physician can be perceived as neglect when, in fact, the family is concerned that the parent may be hospitalized. If hospitals are perceived as places where individuals go to die, as they are among traditional Portuguese, the resistance to professional care is a symbol of love and concern.

The relationship of past experiences to the perception of hospitalization is vividly depicted through its impact on holocaust survivors (Zilberfein and Eskin, 1992). Becoming ill and hospitalized can trigger memories and feelings that affect the ways in which older patients react to their present conditions. The stresses of hospitalization can evoke memories of concentration camps, losses, and threats, which can affect the present recovery process. Although these experiences have been noted among this specific population, they may also occur among other groups who have also undergone traumatic events and suffering. Consequently, the lens through which these individuals perceive the hospital will be greatly colored by their memories.

It is not uncommon for new immigrants to perceive health care systems with feelings of mistrust and anxiety. In the instance of adult children, these feelings often stem from guilt about leaving their parents in the care of the medical system, but, at the same time, they may be translated into anger at the providers (Althausen, 1993). Among Russian immigrants, Althausen found that, in times of the parents' illness or institutionalization, adult children, threatened by feelings of separation and feelings that they are not fulfilling their filial duties, can attempt to manipulate the providers and interfere with the health care plan and process.

Culture can affect the experiences and needs of hospitalized children and their families as well as those of the elderly. High-technology hospital settings with various types of providers and procedures, which often separate parents from ill children, can be extremely stressful to families in which strong cohesion and protectiveness are the norm. As an example, one of the authors, in responding to the needs of a newly arrived Vietnamese family whose infant had a high fever, found a subcompact car not large enough for the ride to the hospital, as the grandparents, aunt and uncle, and siblings demanded to accompany the baby to the emergency ward.

Cultures that emphasize strong maternal nurturing and protection and interdependence among the family members can have difficulties in adjusting to the hospitalization of one of their members. In fact, the hospitalization itself may be interpreted as a failure of the family to attend to its normative obligations of care. Hispanic mothers of hospitalized children often feel guilty that they are not fulfilling their expected roles as nurturers (Gruendelman, 1990).

Hospital discharges, like the hospital experience itself, can also be strongly influenced by ethnicity. Cox (1996) found that families of hospitalized African-American patients with dementia were significantly more likely to plan on taking their relative home than were white families. In addition, the study also found that the African-American families were significantly less satisfied than the white families with the discharge planning process and with their involvement in it.

Institutionalization itself is affected by ethnicity, with minorities continuing to underutilize nursing homes. Studies on African Americans indicate that they are much less likely than whites to desire to place relatives in nursing homes (Hinrichson and Ramirez, 1992). The overall rate of utilization of nursing homes by African Americans is half to three-quarters of that of elderly whites (Liu and Manton, 1989). The possible explanations for this lack of use, such as reduced ability to pay for private care, feelings of discrimination and racism, negative attitudes toward institutions based on previous experiences, and strong informal supports, are associated with ethnic group membership rather than an absence of need.

Terminal care, like hospitalization, has also been associated with cultural differences. Fewer blacks than whites use hospice services even when services are located in black neighborhoods and involve active outreach (Lundgren and Chen, 1986). A study of racial differences in attitudes toward hospice care (Neubauer and Hamilton, 1990) found that blacks were significantly more likely than whites to want to live as long as possible under any circumstances, more likely to think that death should be avoided at all costs, and less likely to want to die at home than in a hospital, and therefore hospice care might be interpreted in their view as "giving up." These attitudes are believed to contribute to the tendency of blacks not to use hospices for care of the terminally ill.

Mental Health

The concept of mental health, like physical health, is perceived through the ethnic lens. Ethnic values, expectations, and attitudes can have a strong influence on how psychological well-being, mental health, and symptoms of mental illness are viewed and, subsequently, the treatment mental problems receive. Giordano (1973) emphasizes the contribution of ethnicity to mental health through its effect on identity. This is particularly true for African Americans, whose encounters with racism can affect their self-concepts and self-esteem (Chestang, 1972).

But, as important as identity is, it is also difficult to separate ethnicity from socioeconomic status in understanding psychological problems. Poverty is a critical factor in depression, and minority groups are more likely to live in poverty. At the same time, the relationship of socioeconomic status to mental health is a complicated one. Porter (1971) found that black working-class children had higher self-esteem than those of the middle class, most likely due to the greater interactions of the latter group with white people and thus their exposure to more racism.

Ethnicity can affect the ways in which individuals cope with stress and mental problems, whether they seek professional care, talk with their families, consult their ministers, or turn to prayer. Thus, studies have indicated that black women and elderly blacks are more likely than others to use prayer and a belief in God as a primary coping mechanism in dealing with problems (Chatters and Taylor, 1989; Wilson-Ford, 1992).

Just as ethnicity can affect the perception of physical symptoms, it affects the perception of mental symptoms and even the identification of symptoms as abnormal. If confusion and hallucinations are perceived as a sign of personal weakness or affliction by an evil spirit, mental health treatment is unlikely to be sought. If confusion among the elderly is not perceived as an illness, caregivers are unlikely to feel a need for assistance. In general, if behaviors are not viewed as abnormal, help is not likely to be sought. The way in which mental health and mental problems are defined and identified will affect the use of mental health counselors.

The ways in which mental problems are perceived influences the choice of treatment. Elderly American Indians frequently somatize their problems, since admitting physical illness is more acceptable than psychological problems, a view that is believed to stem from a consideration of the person as a whole rather than a fragmented being (Neligh and Scully, 1990). Consequently, psychological problems are likely to be taken to the primary care physician. Less acculturated Asian Americans often attribute mental illness to loss of soul, demonic possession, or intervention of spirits and may therefore turn to fortune-tellers or sorcerers for exorcism or prayers (Cheung and Snowden, 1990). Asians who believe in a natural balance, as in ying and yang or hot and cold, may take their distress to herbal doctors or acupuncturists.

Groups may avoid mental health services due to the shame attached to mental problems. Among Chinese, Filipinos, Koreans, and Japanese, mental disorders, juvenile delinquency, AIDS, and poverty are considered shameful and disgraceful to the family (Sue and Morishima, 1982). Many will avoid mental health agencies, since they represent an admission that these problems exist and this could cause loss of face for the entire family. Therefore, even when services are available, they are likely to be underutilized.

However, although cultural values and traditions can influence the use of mental health services, it is essential to recognize that structural and organizational factors may also act as barriers. A major barrier to care is lack of knowledge about mental health services. Many ethnic groups, particularly those who have recently arrived or who come as refugees, are unfamiliar with Western mental health programs or models of care.

The poverty status and limited financial resources of many minority groups are major barriers to service. With limited coverage under public programs or few available services, access to care remains restricted. Thus, even those willing to use these services will find that limited resources limit utilization. Until this major barrier to care is removed, ethnic minorities are likely to remain outside of the service network. Explaining underutilization of services only in terms of cultural preferences or attitudes can be a means of justifying a lack of accessible programs.

The characteristics of the providers themselves, as interpreted through the ethnic lens, can facilitate or deter the utilization of health services. Professionals who do not speak or understand the language of the group may be perceived as reflecting the insensitivity or lack of caring of the program. In addition, patients who are not able to understand English fully will find it difficult to describe their problems or conditions to these persons. These difficulties are often compounded when the professional is the opposite gender or is perceived as being too young by the ethnic patient. These characteristics, which may be of little consequence to most patients, can act as barriers to care for many ethnic persons.

AIDS

Working with persons who have AIDS is a particular concern of social workers, as these individuals frequently face a lack of support systems, unemployment, low income, discrimination, and psychological problems associated with the diagnosis and its prognosis. AIDS has become a primary health problem among blacks and Hispanics, as the proportion of cases among these populations continues to increase while it simultaneously has declined among whites. The epidemic is having a disproportionate effect among racial and ethnic minorities. Between the years 1993 and 1995 the proportion of AIDS cases among whites decreased from 60% to 43%, while the proportion among blacks increased from 25% to 38% and among Hispanics from 14% to 18% (Centers for Disease Control and Prevention, 1995).

The higher prevalence of the disease among minorities is attributed to intravenous drug use and sexual contact with infected drug users. Higher rates of needle sharing among non-white drug users, inability of minority needle users to obtain sterile equipment, and poorer health status of non-white populations in the United States are factors that increase these individuals' risk of contracting AIDS (Peterson and Bakeman, 1989). Poverty, poor nutrition, and inadequate health and education services in ghettos and impoverished ethnic minority communities in the United States contribute to the increase of AIDS among blacks and Hispanics (Lester and Saxxon, 1988). Thus, both social and environmental factors are involved in the spread of the disease, with their greatest impact on ethnic minority populations.

AIDS and the Ethnic Lens

AIDS exemplifies the way in which the ethnic lens affects the perspective by which a problem is viewed and the way in which this perspective can affect future care. One theory of the origin of the disease is that it began in Africa, occurring as a virus in animals like the African green monkey (Essex and Kanki, 1988). The virus was transmitted to humans through sexual contact with these animals or by drinking their blood. The black community views these theories as racist and perceives them as ways to shift the blame for the illness. In fact, among the black community, it is theorized that AIDS is a virus that was engineered to eliminate black people (Greaves, 1994).

Several studies have addressed the way in which minority group status and cultural attitudes are associated with the spread of the illness. Such attitudes affect education about the illness, its prognosis, and the way in which infection occurs. Consequently, with histories of oppression and social discrimination, it is not surprising that one perception of the origin of the illness, through the ethnic lens, is that it is racist and politically motivated by the white community.

African-American and Hispanic AIDS patients tend to come for treatment when the disease is in a more advanced stage, probably as a result of a previous history of poor medical care, a lack of financial resources, and cultural barriers in communicating with health care providers. Additionally, white physicians are often unaware of the differences in dietary practices, the lack of future orientation or long-range planning, or the role of informal supports and kin in health behaviors (Mays and Cochran, 1987). Yet, all of this knowledge is important for clarifying the lens of the professional so that appropriate prevention and treatment can be offered.

Homophobic attitudes are common among African Americans and Hispanics, where the cultural expectation for males is to be "macho" or have "machismo." Given this attitude, homosexuality is perceived as deviant, homosexuals are likely to be ostracized, and homosexuality is likely to be denied. In addition, many black churches, including fundamentalist denominations and some Baptist churches, view homosexuality as sinful and thus have little sympathy for persons with AIDS (Mays and Cochran, 1987). Black gay men with AIDS may be perceived as having received their just punishment.

The negative attitudes that many African Americans have toward AIDS have been viewed as an outcome of the black emphasis on group survival against social pressures from a white-dominated society; homosexuality is a cultural phenomenon of white people (Icard, Schilling, El-Bassel, and Young, 1992). African-American males with the illness are therefore deviant in terms of cultural expectations regarding maleness, as well as in their white behaviors.

But the illness does not affect only minority men. African-American and Hispanic women are the largest segment of females infected with human immunodeficiency virus (HIV)/AIDS in the United States, composing 74% of all reported AIDS cases among women (Novello, 1993). A major contributor to the spread of this disease is unprotected sex. Among both Hispanic and African American men, the use of condoms is traditionally perceived as compromising their virility, with such attitudes seriously compromising the health of the women. Being dependent on the men or belief systems that demean assertiveness increases the risk of infection.

Developing health education programs that are sensitive to cultural beliefs and values is imperative. These programs rely upon health care providers' clear understanding of the way in which the illness is perceived. Social workers need to work toward sensitizing minorities to the realities of the illness and the ways in which it is spread. Social workers can assist in altering attitudes toward homosexuality and health care that blur the ethnic lens and contribute to the risk of AIDS.

Helping health care professionals and others serving AIDS patients to understand the conflicts encountered by ethnic minority persons, which can complicate their care and affect the spread of the disease, is essential. In particular, developing culturally sensitive services for African-American females diagnosed with HIV/AIDS is a special need and a challenge to the social work community as service providers (Dicks, 1994).

Increasing service accessibility by locating services within ethnic communities with care provided by ethnic staff will contribute to utilization. In addition, reducing fragmentation among programs will also facilitate their use. Providing medical care for mothers and babies in one program rather than in separate facilities can contribute to the use of services.

Support groups for patients and their families can be important in helping persons to cope with illness. Social workers can use their knowledge regarding group development and processes in the formation of these groups within ethnic communities. Such groups can help to alleviate the feelings of exclusion and alienation that many may experience, as well as provide practical assistance in dealing with the demands of the illness.

The Ethnic Lens and Social Work Practice

Providing acceptable and accessible health care to ethnic and minority individuals is a prerequisite to the improvement of their health status. Because a key function of social work is to improve individuals' functioning and to help assure that the environment is responsive to individual needs, the discipline has a primary position in the health care field. Working with ethnic communities, institutions, patients, and their families to assure that problems and conditions that affect health and well-being are recognized is a central role of the profession. The effectiveness of this work is dependent upon the clarity of the ethnic lens.

Within the community, health care services must be available and accessible and made acceptable to the populations. This entails having staff who are able to communicate with the patients in their own language. Staff who are knowledgeable about the culture and the ways in which values and norms relate to the concepts of health, illness, and medical care are important links to the health care system. Professional staff of the same ethnic background as the patients can further service utilization, as they are able to interpret the service according to traditions of the group while acting as liaisons between the health care agency and the group.

The complexity of health care systems, both in community centers and hospitals, can itself be a deterrent to care, and it is in this area that the role of the ethnic lens is apparent. For individuals accustomed to more traditional and personal measures of care, for those who view healing as an art rather than a science, the institutional demands associated with much of medical care can be perceived as contradictory to care itself. Social workers' understanding of the way this complexity may be perceived can work personalize these medical systems so that the lens through which they are perceived sees them as meeting the needs.

By acting as links with the bureaucracy, social workers can help to encourage medical care and compliance with regimes. Interpreting and discussing procedures or treatments, assisting persons with complicated forms, and making waiting rooms more comfortable are examples of processes that are critically important to the care of ethnic patients.

The medical model itself, as it focuses on diagnoses, treatment, and cure, can be inappropriate to the needs of many ethnic groups for whom health care is perceived as a more holistic practice involving many areas of the self. Patients who perceive health as a balance among natural forces can be further alienated by a system and practitioners who concentrate only on a specific ailment rather than on the whole person. Effective treatment and patient compliance require practitioners and patients to perceive the problems through a common lens. Social workers can help to assure that the same lens is used by both patients and physicians.

Within hospital settings, discharge planning has become a major task of social workers. Assuring that discharges are appropriate and meet the needs of both the institution and the individual requires intricate planning and consultation. It involves a knowledge of the care needs of the individual patient, an assessment of the living situation (including the informal support system), and thorough knowledge of the available formal supports and resources and the way in which ethnic values can affect the discharge plan. Discharge planners must be careful that the lenses through which they perceive their patients are not distorted by generalizations.

For example, encouraging instititutionalization for persons whose values stress familial care may be perceived by group members as representing lack of caring and insensitivity on the part of the social worker. At the same time, basing a discharge plan on a lens that assumes the family has the ability, resources, and support to continue as caregivers may ignore the particular stresses the family is encountering.

In working with diverse ethnic groups, social workers should assist individuals to understand the ways in which beliefs and behaviors can contribute to their health or illness. In doing this, it is important to demonstrate knowledge about and respect for the group's traditions while indicating how these behaviors may have negative consequences. The success of programs to promote immunization, alter diets, or encourage the use of condoms will be strongly related to the ability of the health care provider to communicate with the ethnic populations.

In assessment of patients, social workers need to determine the extent to which individuals rely on folk medicines, herbs, or healers and the reasons for this reliance. In many instances, persons may turn to folk remedies and healers because of an absence of accessible health care professionals in the community or poor experiences with the health care system. A clear ethnic lens to assist in understanding the reasons for the preference for traditional care is necessary for developing responsive health care services. At the same time, demonstrating understanding and respect for these traditional modes of care can be important to the establishment of the physician-patient relationship.

Social work assessments are important parts of treatment and discharge plans. The assessments of ethnic individuals in health care settings should include their proficiency in English, availability of supports, availability of formal supports and resources, medical insurance, understanding of the medical condition and treatment, use of other types of practitioners, herbs, or medications, and their legal status. This information can help to assure that care is received and maintained.

As discussed in this chapter, family values and roles are often critical in the treatment process. Knowledge of the ways in which specific groups perceive the roles of the family, whether that of parent or adult child, and the stresses that illness or institutionalization can place on those roles is a fundamental part of the helping process. Providing parents with places to sleep in the child's hospital room and relieving adult children of the guilt they may experience in placing a parent in a nursing home are examples of the ways in which social workers can help to increase the acceptability of services.

Improving the health status of minorities necessitates the development of health promotion programs that are sensitive to the specific cultures. Since many of the problems affecting minority health are associated with environmental factors such as poverty, poor nutrition, homicide, and drug abuse, the effectiveness of these programs will depend to a large extent on the attention given to these problems. Consequently, as social workers focus on the stresses that can result from poor interactions with the environment, they can make major contributions to the development of effective health promotion services.

Education is particularly important with regard to mental health. Many ethnic groups are unfamiliar with concepts of mental health and mental health services. Attitudes that see mental problems as shameful, a stigma, or punishment can further deter persons from services. Educating persons regarding the causes of mental problems and assuring them that these problems are not shameful and can be helped are needed. Assuring that materials are relevant to the needs and beliefs of specific populations, are understandable, and can help to clarify the lens of the group with regard to the problems and the roles of providers is basic for service utilization.

Understanding belief systems and the ways in which beliefs affect the perception of symptoms and the decision of whether to seek treatment is a necessary part of care. But, it is equally important to recognize that there is great diversity in adherence to cultural beliefs and their influences on behavior. Without this recognition, social workers and other health professionals are at risk of inappropriately assuming attitudes that may not be valid. The ethnic lens of the practitioner must be able to discern the patient's level of acculturation and willingness to accept the health care plan.

Awareness of the impact of socioeconomic status on illness and disease is essential, because its interactions with environment and lifestyle can be as significant as the effect of culture. The ethnic lens cannot ignore the impact of poverty on health status and behaviors, since its impact on the environment and its resources have overwhelming consequences on the health and well-being of ethnic minority groups. Socioeconomic status can explain much of the racial and ethnic differences in disease because it affects persons through crowding, poor nutrition and sanitation, social stresses, and inadequate medical care (Polednak, 1989). Working toward the correction of these social problems, developing policies, and encouraging the development of services within ethnic communities are important tasks for social workers.

In summary, social workers in health care settings have critical roles to play with regard to the health and service utilization of ethnic groups. The effectiveness of their roles can be critical links to the service system and thus to the increased well-being of these persons. Their own ethnic lenses must be sensitive to the culture and traditions of the group while also not distorted by generalizations. This clarity will be enhanced through their knowledge and understanding and reflected through their respect.

Questions for Discussion

1. In what ways may accessibility to health services affect their use by ethnic groups?
2. Describe the ways in which culture can affect the definition and treatment of illness.
3. Explain the barriers that ethnic group members may encounter in their use of mental health services.
4. Discuss how the ethnic lens affects care and treatment of AIDS.
5. Describe why the medical model may be inappropriate for the care of many ethnic patients.

References

Althausen, L. (1993). Journey of separation: Elderly Russian immigrants and their adult children in the health care setting. *Social Work in Health Care, 19*, 61–75.

Applewhite, S. (1995). Curanderimno: Demystifying the health beliefs and practices of elderly Mexican Americans. *Health and Social Work, 20*, 247–253.

Centers for Disease Control and Prevention. (1995, November). First 500,000 AIDS cases—United States, 1995. *Morbidity and Mortality Weekly Report, 44*(46).

Chatters, L., and Taylor, R. (1989). Life problems and coping strategies of older black adults. *Social Work, 34*, 313–319.

Chestang, L. (1972). *Character Development in a Hostile Environment.* Chicago: University of Chicago Press.

Cheung, F., and Snowden, L. (1990). Community mental health and ethnic minority populations. *Community Mental Health Journal, 20*, 277–291.

Cox, C. (1986). Physician utilization by three groups of ethnic elderly. *Medical Care, 24*, 667–676.

Cox, C. (1996). Outcomes of hospitalization: Factors influencing the discharges of African American and white dementia patients. *Social Work in Health Care, 23*, 23–38.

Delgado, M. (1988). Groups in Puerto Rican spiritism: Implications for clinicians. In C. Jacobs and D. Bowles (Eds.), *Ethnicity and Race: Critical Concepts in Social Work* (pp. 34–47). Silver Spring, MD: National Association of Social Workers.

Dicks, B. (1994). African American women and AIDS: A public health/social work challenge. *Social Work in Health Care, 19*, 123–143.

Essex, M., and Kanki, P. (1988). The origins of the AIDS virus. *Scientific American, 259*, 64–71.

Giordano, J. (1973). *Ethnicity and Mental Health.* New York: American Jewish Committee.

Gold, B., and Socolar, D. (1987). *Report of the Boston Committee on Access to Health Care.* Boston: Boston Committee on Access to Health Care.

Greaves, W. (1994). AIDS and sexually transmitted diseases. In I. Livingston (Ed.), *Handbook of Black American Health* (pp. 157–168). Westport, CT: Greenwood.

Gruendelman, S. (1990). Developing responsiveness to the health needs of Hispanic children and families. In K. Davidson and S. Clarke (Eds.), *Social Work in Health Care: A Handbook for Practice, Part II* (pp. 713–730). Binghamton, NY: Haworth Press.

Hinrichson, G., and Ramirez, M. (1992). African American and white dementia careagivers: A comparison of their adaptation, adjustment and service utilization. *Gerontologist, 32*, 375–381.

Icard, L., Schilling, R., El-Bassel, N., and Young, D. (1992). Preventing AIDS among black gay men and black gay and heterosexual male intravenous drug users. *Social Work, 37*, 440–445.

Lester, C., and Saxxon, L. (1988). AIDS in the Black community: The plague, the politics, the people. *Death Studies, 12*, 563–571.

Liu, K., and Manton, K. (1989) The effects of nursing home use on Medicaid eligibility, *Gerontologist, 29*, 59–66.

Lundgren, L., and Chen, S. (1986). Hospice: Concept and implementation in the Black community. *Journal of Community Health Nursing, 3*, 137–144.

Mays, V., and Cochran, S. (1987). Acquired immunodeficiency syndrome and Black Americans: Special psychological issues. *Public Health Reports, 102*, 224–231.

Mechanic, D. (1978). *Medical Sociology* (2nd ed.). New York: Free Press.

Neligh, G., and Scully, J. (1990). Differential diagnosis of major mental disorders among American Indian elderly. In U.S. Department of Health and Human Services, *Minority Aging* (DHHS Publication No. HRS-P-DV 904). Washington DC: U.S. Government Printing Office.

Neubauer, B., and Hamilton, C. (1990). Racial differences in attitudes toward hospice care. *Hospice Journal, 6*, 37–48.

Novello, A. (1993). The HIV/AIDS epidemic: A current picture. *Journal of Acquired Immune Deficiency Syndrome, 6*, 645–654.

Peterson, J., and Bakeman, R. (1989). AIDS and IV drug use among ethnic minorities. *Journal of Drug Issues, 19*, 27–37.

Polednak, S. (1989). *Racial and Ethnic Differences in Disease.* New York: Oxford University Press.

Porter, J. (1971). *Black Child, White Child: The Development of Racial Attitudes.* Cambridge, MA: Harvard University Press.

Sue, S., and Morishima, J. (1982). *The Mental Health of Asian Americans.* San Francisco: Jossey-Bass.

U.S. Department of Health and Human Services. (1992). *Healthy People 2000: National Health Promotion and Disease Prevention Objectives.* Washington, DC: U.S. Government Printing Office.

Wilson-Ford, V. (1992) Health-protective behaviors of rural black elderly women. *Health and Social Work, 17*, 28–36.

Zborowski, M. (1952). Cultural components in response to pain. *Journal of Social Issues, 8*, 16–30.

Zilberfein, F., and Eskin, V. (1992). Helping holocaust survivors with the impact of illness and hospitalization: Social work role. *Social Work in Health Care, 18*, 59–70.

Zola, I., (1973). Pathways to the doctor—from person to patient. *Social Science and Medicine, 7*, 677–689.

8

Ethnicity and Social Welfare Policy

Social work practice cannot be separated from social policy because policy, to a large extent, determines the way in which practice is carried out. Social policy reflects society's values, which in turn shape services and programs. Since the founding of the United States, much of its social policy and resulting legislation have centered around ethnicity. The early promise of religious freedom that brought many religious and ethnic groups to this country is an illustration of the major role that values and social policy have played in shaping lives and American society. At the same time, the problems confronting these immigrants in their efforts to become American illustrates the complexity of implementing social policy that reflects these values.

Key values in American society, around which the society is centered, have been classified as work, mobility, status, independence, individualism, moralism, and ascription (Tropman, 1989). Added to this list must be the recent concern and discussion over the role of "family values" in American society. The pluralistic nature of American society often impedes a consensus as to the meaning of these values, their relative importance, and the subsequent direction of social policies. In particular, diverse ethnic groups are likely to differ in their adherence to and interpretation of these values.

For example, family values can be interpreted in many ways. Within the Hispanic population, family values may pertain to the entire extended kinship network, while for another group the term may relate only to the nuclear family. For Koreans, the concept of placing the individual first, "individualism," conflicts with that of familism, in which the family is the focus of attention. Developing social policies that can adequately address the needs of all is a major challenge.

Many social policies are enacted which, in themselves, reflect the ambiguity among values. Demanding that mothers on welfare work conflicts with values that stress the importance of family and nurturing care for children. Banning sex education in schools can be viewed as supporting morality but also as threatening to the future status and independence of the adolescent. It is not surprising that the most frustrated by the discrepancies in policies are those who are most depend on them. To a large extent, these are ethnic minority persons.

The social work profession, through its Code of Ethics (National Association of Social Workers, 1980), confirms its own political nature, particularly with regard to the needs of diverse groups. The code charges social workers with the responsibility of acting to prevent discrimination, ensuring that all persons have equal access to resources and opportunities (with special regard for the disadvantaged and oppressed), expanding choices for the oppressed, promoting conditions that encourage respect for diversity, and advocating for changes to improve social conditions and promote social justice. Underlying these mandates is the overriding concern that social policy act to assure equal access to society and its institutions for all groups.

This access is easier in periods of expansion and economic growth, when the labor of ethnic and minority persons is greatly needed. However, even this access is limited and, thus, groups may secure employment but still find themselves excluded in other areas of society. Moreover, the cheap labor that these outsiders offer is easily exploited so that the group itself benefits little. During periods of economic slowdown or decline, American social policy has tended to become more exclusionary as the "outsiders" are no longer needed. In extreme conditions, ethnic groups are at risk of being perceived as responsible for the decline.

Policy and Equality

Although all Americans are guaranteed equal protection under the Constitution and the country was founded on the belief that all persons are created equal, "equal" was interpreted as separate. Until the middle of the 20th century, social policy and legislation were supportive of segregation in schools, on public buses, and in other public places. It was not until 1954 that the Supreme Court ruled that separate was not equal and that "segregation retarded the education and mental development of Negro children." This major ruling laid the framework for the civil rights movement of the 1960s, which brought the issue of racial exploitation sharply into view and led to the Civil Rights Act of 1964.

The Civil Rights Act is the major legislative reform attempting to assure racial and ethnic equality. Among its measures are the banning of discrimination or segregation on the basis of race, color, religion, or national origin in public places and in employment by those employing 25 or more persons and the ending of discrimination in any program or activity receiving federal funds. Subsequent amendments in 1968 prohibited discrimination in housing. These policies set the framework for including in the greater society those who had been, until then, commonly excluded.

However, the actual impact of the act in improving the lives of the disenfranchised is debatable. The socioeconomic status of African Americans, Mexican Americans, Puerto Ricans, Native Americans, and Alaskan Natives in comparison with others in American society remains low. Indeed, the fact that disproportionate numbers of these populations are in poverty is in itself evidence that discrimination continues.

Affirmative Action

The affirmative action programs enacted in the 1960s were both a consequence of the civil rights movement and a direct federal response to discrimination in employment and education. Under an executive order signed by President Johnson in 1965, all contractors receiving federal money had to follow affirmative action guidelines, which ensured that applicants' race, creed, color, or national origin were not considered in applications.

Affirmative action moved beyond the issue of prohibiting discrimination. It became more aggressive by requiring that there be plans that identified the steps taken to assure that preferential treatment be given to groups who had previously been discriminated against in employment. In order to increase minority enrollment, the Equal Employment Act of 1972 applied the same principles to colleges and universities.

Controversy has ensued over affirmative action policies. Proponents view the programs as essential for promoting equal opportunity and outcomes. The policies are a means to assuring that the institutions of the country reflect the diversity of the population, thereby guaranteeing the inclusion of all groups. Opponents deride the programs as utilizing quotas and contributing to reverse discrimination, particularly against white males. Affirmative action is viewed as discriminatory and exclusive, as it gives preference to minorities while jeopardizing the opportunities of the majority. Preferential treatment for minorities is viewed as reverse discrimination against whites and a major threat to their well-being.

Within education, proponents of affirmative action assert that schools and universities must represent the diversity of the population and that college education must be available to all ethnic groups. Affirmative action policies are essential in order to meet and serve group needs, to assure groups' integration into society, and to meet the changing requirements of an increasingly diverse society.

At the same time, critics contend that the policy permits the admission of lesser qualified minority students while taking away places from nonminority applicants. In addition, the policy itself is eroded because it fails to distinguish among minority applicants. Institutions seeking minority representation can accept applicants from professional, middle-class backgrounds rather than those who have been truly disadvantaged.

Others see affirmative action policies as further dividing society, for they place groups into competition. From this perspective, the policies can actually undermine minorities by devaluing the qualifications of many individuals who would have been accepted according to their own merit. According to these critics, affirmative action harms, rather than helps, minorities.

At least part of the controversy surrounding affirmative action reflects concerns over whether it presents the best means for overcoming racism and discrimination. From one perspective, its attempts to secure inclusion further divide society. From the other perspective, it is essential for overcoming the barriers that have traditionally prevented equal opportunity and participation for minority groups.

For others, affirmative action is undesirable because it prevents the formation of multiracial political coalitions (Pincus, 1994). These coalitions are necessary for forming the basis for universalistic policies such as a national public works program, which would benefit everyone. Given these policies, affirmative action would no longer be necessary.

Poverty and Welfare

Central to much of the current political debate and attention is the issue of welfare and government's role and responsibility in providing for those who are unable to provide for themselves. As dependency and unemployment are stigmatized in this society, those on welfare are easily perceived as deviant and unworthy. Given the depressed economic conditions of blacks and Hispanics in this country, they are disproportionately on welfare, a condition that gives rise to negative ethnic and racial attitudes and stereotypes.

Blacks and Hispanics are more likely to be in poverty than are whites and to remain in poverty for longer periods. In 1991 and 1992, 3.2% of whites were poor, in comparison with 15.7% of African Americans and 11.8% of Hispanics (U.S. Bureau of the Census, 1995). Almost half, 40.3%, of those persons counted as poor for at least 24 months were African Americans, indicating that, once in poverty, they are likely to remain there.

Poverty is particularly visible among minority children. In 1991 the poverty rate among all children was 17% while it was approximately 46%, among African Americans, 40% among Hispanics, and 38% among Native Americans (Reddy, 1993; U.S. House of Representatives, 1993). Children have become the majority of the poor in the United States, and minority children, African Americans and Hispanics, compose a disproportionate percentage of this population.

Contributing to this poverty is the large proportion of these children living with single mothers. In 1991, 68% of female-headed African-American and Hispanic families and 47% of white female-headed families were living in poverty (U.S. House of Representatives, 1993). Raised in poverty, minority children are easily alienated from society, being deprived of access to the institutions and opportunities available to the nonpoor. Poor nutrition, inadequate housing, and lower quality schools are factors that will affect them throughout their lives.

Although whites compose the majority of persons (57.9%) receiving government assistance through means-tested programs (Aid to Families with Dependent Children [AFDC], food stamps, general assistance, SSI, subsidized housing, and Medicaid), disproportionately large percentages of African Americans (24.2%) and Hispanics (18.9%) are dependent on welfare, as compared with 5.8% of whites (U.S. Bureau of the Census, 1995). This poverty persists even with major cash subsidies through AFDC and Old Age Survivors and Disability Insurance (OASDI) and with in-kind payments such as food stamps, Medicaid, housing assistance, and child nutrition programs. Even with these payments, combined with food stamps, only two states gave sufficient benefits to raise recipients above the poverty threshold (U.S. House of Representatives, 1993).

The high proportions of minority groups in poverty and dependent on welfare mean that social policy focusing on welfare reform has a major impact on their lives. In fact, the large proportions of these persons on welfare strengthens negative stereotypes. The dependency of these minority groups symbolizes their disparity with traditional American values such as work, status, and independence. At the same time, these values are often meaningless to those to whom ascribed characteristics and status dictate their receipt of resources and their place in society.

Anderson (1993) describes African-American youths as caught in a web of persistent poverty. Within this web, there is little hope for a good job, economic security, or a conventional family life. Thus, adherence to the values of those outside of the web is meaningless. With little prospect of employment, it is impossible to support a family. Manhood and status are determined by the number of children the boy has fathered. Girls, caught in the same web, see the baby as offering a measure of independence through welfare, which can permit them to establish their own households. The web therefore perpetuates itself and is likely to continue until jobs and prospects for economic self-sufficiency become a reality.

Values also dominate welfare policy. Allen-Meares and Roberts (1995) view public assistance policy as driven by belief in the work ethic, the family ethic, the nuclear family, and the capitalist processes. Therefore, recipients of assistance are perceived as deviant because they do not conform to these values by being dependent and not working, by not being caretakers of husbands and children, by not being part of a nuclear family, and by not succeeding economically. Consequently, much of the ideology behind public assistance policy blames the high rates of poverty among single female–headed households on unemployment (failure to adhere to the work ethic) and having a nontraditional family structure (failure to function according to the family ethic).

In their review of public assistance policy between 1935, when AFDC was begun, and 1988, Allen-Meares and Roberts (1995) find the objectives for the program dramatically changed. The original beneficiaries were to be dependents of widows or women with disabled husbands who could no longer work. The program was both work and family oriented, thus reflecting important social values.

After World War II, the beneficiaries changed, with a substantial increase in families headed by females who had never been married. In addition, even with prosperity and economic growth, the numbers of participants increased. The result has been a change in objectives, with a focus now on reducing dependency by moving persons into the labor force.

Current debate over welfare reform involves interest in limiting or even reducing payments to persons having more children while on AFDC, limiting the time of eligibility to two years, and denying benefits to those who do not accept employment. The policy is predicated on the perception that persons receiving welfare are irresponsible, unproductive, and involved in undesirable behaviors that keep them dependent. In fact, discussions over welfare policies often revolve more around the behaviors of those on welfare than on the level of public assistance benefits.

The Family Support Act of 1988 requires single mothers of young children older than age 3 to either work or prepare for employment as a requisite for AFDC payments. The act enforces child support through automated tracking of absent parents and the withholding of wages, mandates states to give AFDC benefits to two-parent families (with certain restrictions), and provides child care for parents involved in job training programs. It thus attempts to support both family and work ethics.

However, the ability of the act to reach its intended objectives is severely curtailed by low levels of funding and minimal efforts at skill development and supports. Single mothers will remain near or below the poverty line even if they work at full-time jobs, because of low wages, work interruptions, lack of fringe benefits, and the high cost of child care (U.S. General Accounting Office, 1992). Consequently, although the act may contribute to the opportunities of some, in itself it is unlikely to make a major dent in poverty or the welfare status of minority persons.

The Elderly

Nowhere is the impact of social policy greater than on the lives of ethnic elderly. The conditions contributing to the vulnerability and poorer status of ethnic minority individuals throughout the life span are magnified among the elderly. Whereas 10% of the white population over the age of 65 are poor, 34% of the African-American elderly population and 23% of the Hispanic elderly are poor (U.S. Bureau of the Census, 1995). With increasing age, the difference becomes even more dramatic, with 44% of African Americans over the age of 75 being poor, compared with 17% of the white population.

As found among the younger populations, this poverty is associated with an absence of private health insurance and thus means a greater proportion of income going to out-of-pocket expenditures on health care. Although larger proportions of poor elderly African Americans (39%), and Hispanics, (51%), receive Medicaid than do whites, there are still many low-income elderly who do not qualify for benefits but are still in need of assistance (Sotomayor, 1993; U.S. General Accounting Office, 1992). Strict state requirements and Medicaid's association with being a welfare program create barriers to the use of the program.

Income and retirement policies, health care policies such as Medicare and Medicaid, and even policies regarding publicly assisted housing have major ramifications for the ethnic elderly. As an example, raising the retirement age to 67 means a longer wait for benefits for those who retire early. As early retirement is common among Mexican Americans, this could place a particular strain on their incomes (Stanford, Happersett, and Morton, 1991). At the same time, as minority individuals have shorter life spans than nonminority whites, they collect fewer social security benefits. Whether functional or chronological age should be used in determining eligibility for benefits is a key policy issue.

The most comprehensive policy designed specifically for the elderly is found in the Older Americans Act (OAA) enacted in 1965. Although its original objectives were very broad, they provided for a wide array of services to assist the elderly to remain in the community. The act has continued to be amended, and, since 1973, these amendments have focused on providing services for the most vulnerable of the elderly, those with the greatest social needs. These needs include language barriers and cultural or social isolation caused by racial or cultural barriers, therefore recognizing the particular effect that ethnicity can have on the lives of older persons. The 1978 amendments recognized the specific needs of elderly Native Americans and granted tribes the right to request specific funding for services under the OAA.

As an example of the way in which services address these differences, nutrition programs offered under OAA frequently provide meals compatible with the culture of the group. In one city in California, kitchens prepared lunches for Korean, Mexican, Portuguese, Jewish, Vietnamese, Polish, and Chinese elderly. This type of sensitivity is essential for increasing service participation.

Although the aims of the OAA are laudable, focusing as they do on the needs of the elderly, with particular attention to the minority elderly in the community, the effectiveness of the policy in meeting needs is sharply restricted by the limited funding for its programs. Programs are seldom funded to the extent that they can have a real impact on the lives of the elderly. Indeed, constrained budgets have jeopardized many of the services offered under OAA. In addition, opponents of targeting programs to low-income minority persons are concerned that it is done at the expense of nonminority, low-income elderly and would have this focus removed from legislation.

The needs of the ethnic elderly are often not recognized by service providers since they are among those least likely to make demands or advocate for themselves. In addition, there is often a perception by practitioners that these persons are adequately cared for by their families and thus have little need for social work services. However, the process of assimilation and acculturation and the stresses accompanying it can severely weaken traditional support patterns.

Although many families do assume the care for the elderly and provide extensive support, it is simplistic to assume that this support is consistently available. For many elderly, this support is lacking or is offered only with a great deal of stress. Studies of the care of Alzheimer's patients by black and Hispanic families indicate that these relatives are often extremely burdened and in need of support themselves (Cox and Monk, 1996). Moreover, the greater dependency among African-American and Hispanic older women can actually contribute to a deterioration in family relationships (Markides, 1989).

Basing social policies for the care of the ethnic elderly on myths that presuppose strong informal support systems can severely ignore the real needs of these populations. To be most effective, policy must not be distorted by beliefs that fail to recognize the problems and stresses confronting these persons and their caregivers.

Welfare Reform

In 1996, with the passage of the new welfare reform law, the federal government consolidated the previously existing AFDC, emergency assistance, and Jobs Opportunities and Basic Skills (JOBS) into a Temporary Assistance for Needy Families (TANF) block grant program to the states. Under TANF states are able to determine their own eligibility criteria and benefit levels for individuals, but recipients are limited to no more than two years of benefits without working. In addition, there is a five-year lifetime limit on welfare benefits to adults.

The role of work as a means toward independence and self-sufficiency is particularly emphasized. Persons refusing to work or participate in a work program may have their benefits reduced or terminated. By the year 2002, states must have at least 50% of their single-parent welfare caseloads working at least thirty hours per week or have their block grants reduced by at least 5%. In an effort to promote the important values of families and family responsibility, teenage parents are required to live with their parents or other adult relatives.

Under the reform act, legal immigrants are prohibited from receiving food stamps or Supplementary Security Income (SSI) for five years after entry into the United States. States can determine whether or not to provide Medicaid or TANF to immigrants, but, again, these are not available until the persons have been in the country for at least five years.

The limit on benefits continues to suggest that those on welfare are not working due to a lack of interest on their part. It fails to recognize that the reasons people may not find work is that there are no jobs or that their training is inadequate. In addition, the jobs they find are not necessarily going to take them out of poverty.

In particular, there is concern over the time limit for benefits, since the problems associated with welfare must include "an overhaul of the schools, community-based services to combat gangs and violence, and housing initiatives to enable the poor to live in clean and safe dwellings" (Haveman, 1995, p. 189). Time limits can be effective only if there is real support of the programs, which can make persons independent and self-sufficient. Unfortunately, if persons in the programs do not succeed, their failures can be used as further evidence of entrenched negative attitudes and behaviors.

The impact of the reforms on immigrants is likely to be very severe. After having paid taxes, trusted the system, and abided by its rules, many may find that they are not entitled to benefits such as SSI, a program on which many elderly are dependent.

Immigration and Social Policy

Immigrants come to the United States for many reasons: political or religious freedom, economics, or to be united with their relatives. In the 18th and early part of the 19th centuries, when the country was growing and industry was developing and there was a pressing need for settlers and new workers, there were no restrictions on immigration.

However, between 1875 and 1965, immigration policy became selective, with racism rather than economic needs becoming major contributing factors (Hraba, 1994). Most notably, laws and regulations were passed in the late 1800s that restricted the entry of Chinese, particularly Chinese laborers, into the country. This was followed by limitations on Japanese immigration in the early 1900s.

The Immigration Act of 1917 further discriminated against ethnic groups in that it included a provision that all immigrants had to prove their literacy in order to be admitted. This served to restrict immigration of southern and eastern Europeans while having little impact on northern and western Europeans. The Johnson Act of 1921 actually assigned quotas to immigrants by limiting their numbers to 3% of the nationality living in the United States in 1910. This effectively restricted the numbers of southern and eastern Europeans eligible for entry.

The restrictive policies reflected the attitudes of many Americans toward specific ethnic groups. Southern and eastern European immigrants were viewed as ignorant, with low living standards that created slums, unemployment, and crime; hostile to the Protestant religion; and a threat to established American culture and society (Bennett, 1963). Limiting their entry was a means of ensuring the security of America's boundaries and of society itself.

The Quota Act of 1924 lowered the proportion of persons eligible for immigration from 3% to 2%, based on the 1890 census. In addition, quotas were placed on national origins, causing further restrictions from southern and eastern Europe. It was not until 1965 that national quotas on immigrants were replaced by international ones. The law set a uniform quota of 20,000 immigrants per country outside of the Western Hemisphere and placed a ceiling on immigration from the Western Hemisphere. The act also established preferences for immigrants based on family unification and particular skill.

Between 1945 and 1990, one quarter of all immigrants to the United States were admitted on humanitarian grounds (Fix and Passel, 1994). The Refugee Act of 1980 allowed into the country persons who could show a fear of persecution in their own country by indicating that return to the country would be dangerous. The act has had particular influence on the entry of Southeast Asians, Cubans, Haitians, and Russian Jews. Under this act, refugees are eligible for benefits such as Medicaid and welfare assistance.

The act also distinguishes those seeking asylum from refugees. Refugees normally apply for admission overseas, whereas asylum seekers usually petition after having entered the country illegally. Those wanting to leave a country due to poverty or other hardships are considered to be asking for asylum and are not necessarily eligible for the welfare and health benefits available to refugees.

In the last few years, the issue of immigration has been dominated by concerns over the entry of illegal immigrants crossing the border from Mexico. Although these persons provide cheap labor in agriculture, some believe that they take jobs away from Americans. Debate also revolves around health care costs and education for the children of illegal immigrants and whether these costs are offset by the money they spend in the country.

The 1986 Immigration Reform and Control Act was enacted as a means of controlling illegal immigration. Under the act, undocumented persons who had been in the country continuously since 1982 were given 1 year in which to apply for amnesty. Those living in the country since 1972 could receive residency without amnesty. This law also imposes fines on employers hiring illegal immigrants, with some exemptions for those in agriculture. Consequently, the law seeks to control illegal immigration by restricting these immigrants' ability to work.

The Immigration Act of 1990 increased legal immigration ceilings by 40%. However, much of this increase is designated to highly skilled immigrants. It also establishes temporary protected status for those living in the United States who are jeopardized by armed conflicts or disasters in their native countries.

These immigration policies give sustenance to the perceptions of ethnic groups and their appropriateness to American society. For the most part, the policies have tended to favor groups viewed as being able to contribute to the country's needs and who have characteristics most compatible with the majority population. These persons will be easily integrated into society and able to contribute to it.

Conversely, policies have served to restrict those perceived as culturally different and possible threats to the established order. Restrictions on these persons are most severe when the economy is seen as not being able to absorb them. Beliefs that they will further drain the country through their demands on welfare and social programs are further influences toward restrictive policies, particularly when the economy lacks a need for their skills.

Health Care Policy

As discussed earlier in this book, ethnic groups have varying orientations to health and health care and different experiences with the health care system. Given these differences, they all require available and accessible medical services. Health care policy provides the important framework for this accessibility. The limitations of the current health care system and its need for reform have become a major political issue. In particular, the high proportion of persons without medical insurance, even among the employed, has drawn national attention.

The health care of ethnic and minority groups will not be significantly improved unless policies effectively remove the many barriers that prevent their access to the health care system. This includes increased coverage by medical insurance, health education and health promotion programs that are sensitive to specific ethnic groups and their problems, and professionals who understand ethnic values and traditions that affect health status and use of services.

The issue of minority health and the disparity among groups was officially recognized in 1990 with the passage of Public Law 101-527, which was designed to improve the health of minority individuals. The law recognizes the many factors contributing to health and health care, including the poorer health status among the disadvantaged and the relationship of this status to the health of minority groups, the high rates of chronic illness and infant mortality among minority populations, and the need for more minority professionals in the health care field.

Health insurance has become a major policy issue for the nation, but it has particular significance for ethnic minority populations. African Americans and Hispanics are more likely than non-Hispanic whites to lack health insurance and to be in situations that are most frequently associated with a lack of insurance.

Data from the 1993 population survey reveal that 15% of the population have no health insurance. However, whereas only 15% of the white population are uninsured, 23% of the black and 34% of the Hispanic population are uninsured (Employee Benefits Research Institute, 1995). In addition, nearly half of the blacks and Hispanics without insurance were poor, while only 20% of the uninsured whites were poor. More of the uninsured blacks than either whites or Hispanics were nonworking poor (Short, Cornelius, and Goldstone, 1990).

Health insurance is a foundation for access to health services because it is related to having a regular source of care, using health services, and making more physician visits (Lefkowitz and Monheit, 1993). In this regard, public insurance such as Medicaid is as significant as private insurance as a contributor to health service utilization. In 1987, 86% of those with private insurance and 87% of those with public insurance alone used health services, as compared with only 64% of those with no insurance.

Access to care involves more than insurance coverage. It also includes having a regular source of care and services that are relatively convenient to use. Again, these measures also indicate the extent to which minorities are at a disadvantage in this society. African Americans and Hispanics are twice as likely as whites to use hospital outpatient departments, emergency rooms, and facilities other than physicians' offices as their usual sources for medical care (Cornelius, Beauregard, and Cohen, 1991). Minorities are also more likely than whites to travel an hour or more to their source of care and to wait over an hour for assistance.

These findings have major implications for health care policy as it attempts to address the needs of the population. The disparity in the health care system with regard to minorities is a vivid indicator of the way in which social policy affects the lives and well-being of ethnic groups. Reducing costs and assuring equal access to care are the goals of health reform. Encouraging and enabling persons to receive preventive care and treatment at the beginning stages of an illness could significantly reduce the expenses associated with treating the illness in its more advanced states

Interracial Adoptions

Although the issue of interracial adoptions does not have the magnitude of a social problem, like the other issues discussed here, it does illustrate the way in which perspectives regarding ethnic identity and culture can directly influence policy. The issue of primary debate and concern is whether the adoption of African-American or Asian children by white parents erodes their sense of identity and thus threatens their cultural heritage. In the extreme, the permanent placement of black children in white homes is perceived as racial and cultural genocide and a hostile act against the black community (Merritt, 1985).

On the other hand, research by Simon and Altstein (1987) claims that there are no data to support the belief that transracial adoptions are detrimental to either the child, the adoptive parents, or the siblings. Their findings from a longitudinal study of families adopting a non-white child show that parents and children feel good about themselves and about their relationships with each other. Parents would do it again, felt that they had done well with their children, and would recommend it to others. The children, all adolescents, felt committed to their parents and families, with the overpowering feeling that love is what matters most.

Presently, the policy, under challenge in many jurisdictions, is to avoid transracial adoptions. The governing policy of most child welfare agencies is to place children with parents of the same race or to maintain them in foster care. Thus, with a shortage of minority families seeking adoptions, many children are left without permanent placement. Fears that the ethnic identity of the child will be eroded and that transracial adoptions will threaten the continuation of the culture have been major influences on the policies of child welfare agencies toward placement.

The policy of denying interracial adoptions, as with other social policies, reflects particular group values. In this instance, the adoptions are viewed as racial genocide threatening both the children and their heritage. In our framework, these beliefs and attitudes have shaped the lens through which policy makers and practitioners perceive the adoptions and their potential outcomes. As with other social policies, a closer scrutiny of the existing data and further studies on the outcomes of the adoptions could result in a more equitable policy for both children and adopting parents.

Policy and the Ethnic Lens

As illustrated in this chapter, much of social policy is based upon attitudes, beliefs, and even stereotypes about ethnic populations. The history of immigration to this country as well as the approaches to welfare, illustrate the way policy can be used as a means of legislating and enacting these beliefs.

Although some of the work of policy formation is not within the realm of social work, it is social work practitioners who are often charged with enforcing these policies through practice. It therefore becomes the responsibility of the profession to assure that the policies are just and will effectively meet the problems they seek to solve. Good social work practice necessitates a dual awareness that entails social workers' understanding of how policy affects practice and practice contributes to policy (Briar and Briar, 1982).

The implications of this awareness are particularly strong in practice with ethnic populations. Perceiving groups through an ethnic lens that is clouded by stereotypes and preconceived attitudes can undermine the development of appropriate policies, because the many factors contributing to the problem are obscured. For example, if adolescent pregnancy among African Americans is perceived as a failure by their own parents to control their behavior, policy will be aimed at developing programs that teach parenting skills. If it is perceived as a way for girls to obtain welfare, policy will aim to deter or prevent payments, and if it is perceived as occurring due to an absence of information on contraception, the policy may be to increase birth control education.

Stereotypes based on discriminatory and even racist attitudes have unfortunately played a major role in social policy. Because policy is so closely integrated with practice, social workers must be sensitive to the ways in which these attitudes affect their work and the lives of their clients. This can only be achieved when their own ethnic lens, rather than reflecting the same attitudes, is able to discern clearly the factors and issues confronting the ethnic group.

Social policies are major influences on the educational and employment opportunities available to ethnic and minority groups and thus can be critical avenues for their integration into societies. Given the poverty of minority populations, policies toward health and welfare have a critical impact on their lives. Social workers have critical roles to play in assuring that these policies are responsive to the diversity of these individuals and their needs.

Social policy reflects the values held toward ethnic groups, but, at the same time, it can also shape the groups' values and behaviors. Policies that discriminate and deter access for specific populations to the resources and benefits available to others can lead to the group's developing behaviors adaptable to their restricted environment. Moreover, if these behaviors are perceived negatively by the greater society, they can be used as further justification for discrimination. If schools in ghetto areas have overcrowded classrooms, poor textbooks, and less-qualified teachers, students may be prone to truancy and may show little interest in attending school. These behaviors may be used as evidence of an innate lack of concern for education and achievement.

This chapter has described some of the major policy areas affecting ethnic populations in which the knowledge and skills of social workers can contribute to social policy. Each of these areas involves practice settings, which implement social policies that have major effects on ethnic groups. In public welfare programs, in work with new immigrants, in health care, in work with the elderly, and in adoptions social work policy must recognize the diverse needs and perspectives of those it is attempting to serve.

So long as the ethnic lens of the policy maker distorts minorities on welfare into cultural stereotypes, it will be difficult to improve their situations effectively. These policies require adequate funding and commitment through many types of programs that improve the overall living standards and situations of these persons. Social workers, through awareness and knowledge of the issues confronting minority groups, can contribute significantly to the development of these policies.

The relevance of social policy to practice is immediately evident to practitioners as they find themselves dealing with problems that have their basis in policies. For many, the first recognition of the impact of policy on practice with ethnic groups is within the agency itself. Social workers can become extremely discouraged as they see clients who speak little English struggling to complete forms that they do not understand. Workers are often frustrated when agency policy demands that children be interviewed alone, when they know that this process conflicts with the family's traditional cultural values and will possibly destroy the family's trust in them.

Working toward change to insure that policies recognize diverse needs and values is a fundamental responsibility for those serving ethnic populations. This can involve advocating for those being ignored or misunderstood by the system to insure that misconceptions and stereotypes do not act as barriers to their receipt of service. Requiring a Mexican-American mother to have proof of her child's vaccinations prior to participating in a Head Start Program could easily be interpreted by her as an initial step toward deportation. Rather than participating in the program, she is likely to keep her child out. In this instance, an understanding of the reasons for her behavior is a first step toward a policy change.

Assuring that myths do not cloud the ethnic lens is essential for policy and program effectiveness. As long as the lens of policy makers is clouded by myths regarding the strength and capability of ethnic families in providing support to the elderly, policies that can strengthen needed support services will not be developed. As practitioners work with these families, they can challenge the validity of these myths by their recognition of the stresses encountered by these families. This identification is important for sensitizing policy makers and subsequent policy change.

Advocating for those who cannot advocate for themselves and working with those who can, but who lack the skills, is another way in which social workers can become involved in policy change. Empowering those who have been disenfranchised to make their needs and demands known to those in political office can be the basis for policy change. As an example, programs that have organized groups of minority elderly persons to campaign for new community services in their areas have been particularly effective in obtaining their objectives.

Social work advocacy is also needed in the political arena, where policies are commonly formed. Professional lobbying for legislation that is perceptive about ethnic groups' concerns and needs and that responds to them is essential. This type of involvement can work toward resolving the inequities resulting from policies based on negative stereotypes.

In addition to participating in policy formation, social workers must also be involved in determining the policy's effectiveness, assessing whether the policies are effectively meeting the needs of clients. The worker's knowledge of the group's culture and traditions is critical for understanding the impact of the policy. As an example, a requirement that persons register for work or training in order to receive services can fail according to the way it is perceived through the ethnic lens. In groups valuing autonomy and self-determination, the requirement can be perceived as punitive. In groups concerned about their legal status, it can be perceived as a basis for deportation. The ethnic knowledge of the professionals can help to identify the weaknesses of the policy that prevent it from reaching its goals.

Policy remains the major means for intervening in and bettering the lives of ethnic populations. The profession's concern with social justice demands that social workers become involved in shaping policies that are sensitive to and respectful of ethnic differences and needs. As social policy in this country remains in ferment, at both the federal and local levels, there is an immense opportunity for social workers to make major contributions to the development of a more just society by working toward assuring that these policies reflect core social work values.

Questions for Discussion

1. Discuss the major criticisms of affirmative action and the views of its proponents.
2. Describe the effectiveness of policies in reducing poverty among minorities.
3. Discuss and give examples of how immigration policies reflect society's perceptions of ethnic groups.
4. Identify the most prominent barriers to health care for ethnic groups and the ways these barriers may be overcome.
5. Give examples of situations in which ethnic stereotypes have affected social policies.

References

Allen-Meares, P., and Roberts, E. (1995). Public assistance in family policy: Closing off options for poor families. *Social Work, 40*, 559–565.

Anderson, E. (1993). Sex codes and family life among poor inner-city youths. In W. Wilson (Ed.), *The Ghetto Underclass: Social Science Perspectives* (pp. 76–95). Newbury Park, CA: Sage.

Bennett, M. (1963). *American Immigration Policies*. Washington, DC: Public Affairs Press.

Briar, K., and Briar, S. (1982). Clinical social work and public policies. In M.A. Mahaffery and J. Hanks (Eds.), *Practical Politics: Social Work and Political Responsibility* (pp. 45–54). Silver Spring, MD: National Association of Social Workers.

Cornelius, L., Beauregard, K., and Cohen, J. (1991). *Usual sources of medical care and their characteristics, 1987* (AHCPR Publicaton No. 91-0042, National Medical Expenditure, Survey Research Findings 11, Agency for Health Care Policy and Research). Rockville, MD: Public Health Service.

Cox, C., and Monk, A. (1996). Strain among caregivers: Comparing the experiences of African American and Hispanic caregivers of Alzheimer's relatives. *International Journal of Aging and Human Development, 43*, 1–9.

Employee Benefits Research Institute. (1995). *Sources of Health Insurance and Characteristics of the Uninsured: Analysis of March 1994 Current Population Survey*, (Issue Brief 158). Washington, DC: Author.

Fix, M., and Passel, J. (1994). *Immigration and Immigrants: Setting the Record Straight.* Washington DC: Urban Institute Press.

Haveman, R. (1995). The Clinton alternative to "Welfare as We Know It": Is it possible? In D. Nightengale and R. Haveman (Eds.), *The Work Alternative: Welfare Reform and the Realities of the Job Market* (pp. 185–190). Washington, DC: Urban Institute Press.

Hraba, J. (1994). *American Ethnicity* (2nd ed.). Itasca, IL: F. E. Peacock.

Lefkowitz, D., and Monheit, A. (1993). *Health Insurance, Use of Health Services, and Health Care Expenditures* (DHHS Publication NO. PHS 92-0017, Medical Expenditure Survey Research Findings, 12, Agency for Health Care Policy and Research). Rockville, MD: Public Health Service.

Markides, K. (1989). Consequences of gender differentials in life expectancy for Black and Hispanic Americans. *International Journal of Aging and Human Development, 29*, 95–102.

Merritt, W. (1985). National Association of Black Social Workers, testimony before Congress, June 25.

National Association of Social Workers. (1980). *Code of Ethics of the National Association of Social Workers.* Silver Spring, MD: Author.

Pincus, F. (1994). The case for affirmative action. In F. Pincus and H. Ehrlich (Eds.), *Race and Ethnic Conflict* (pp. 368–382). Boulder, CO: Westview Press.

Reddy, M. (1993). *Statistical Record of Native North Americans.* Detroit: Gale Research.

Short, P., Cornelius, L., and Goldstone, D. (1990). Health insurance of minorities in the United States. *Journal of Health Care for Poor and Underserved, 1*, 9–24.

Simon, R., and Altstein, H. (1987). *Transracial Adoptees and Their Families: A Study of Identity and Committment.* New York: Praeger.

Sotomayor, M. (1993). The Latino elderly: A policy agenda. In M. Sotomayor and

A. Garcia (Eds.), *Elderly Latinos: Issues and Solutions for the 21st Century* (pp. 1–16). Washington, DC: National Hispanic Council on Aging.

Stanford, E., Happersett, C., and Morton, D. (1991). Early retirement and functional impairment from a muli-ethnic perspective. *Research on Aging, 13*, 5–38.

Tropman, J. (1989). *American Values and Social Welfare*. Englewood Cliffs, NJ: Prentice Hall.

U.S. Bureau of the Census. (1992). *Statistical Abstract of the United States*. Washington, DC: U.S. Government Printing Office.

U.S. Bureau of the Census. (1995). *Poverty in the United States* (Current Population Reports, Series P-60, N. 175). Washington DC: U.S. Government Printing Office.

U.S. General Accounting Office. (1992). *Mother-Only Families: Low Earnings Will Keep Many Children in Poverty.* Washington, DC: Author.

U.S. House of Representatives, Committee on Ways and Means. (1993). *Overview of Entitlement Programs: 1993 Greenbook*. Washington, DC: Author.

9

Conclusions

This book has examined and traced the ways in which ethnicity affects social work practice with individuals, families, groups, and communities, and its roles in the development of social policy and in the area of health. Our intent was not to attempt to cover all of the areas in which social workers are engaged but to specify within certain major areas of practice the types of knowledge and skills necessary for effective interventions with members of ethnic groups.

Indeed, our intent was to explore ethnicity generically, rather than to examine specific group traits and characteristics. The position we have taken is that there are common elements shared by all ethnic groups. These elements affect clients, social workers, and service systems. Certainly, groups are unique in their histories, demography, traditions, and culture. Overriding this uniqueness are shared characteristics that can affect all ethnic individuals and their interactions with the greater society.

We are also cognizant of the diversity within ethnic groups, but we believe that attempting to describe each group individually is impractical and can, in fact, invite stereotyping. Instead, we encourage each social work practitioner to assume the responsibility of applying the general principles and model discussed in the preceding chapters in their perception and understanding of the ethnic populations with which they work.

As shown throughout the chapters, the entire help-seeking and help-giving process is itself influenced by ethnicity. Ethnicity contributes to the ways in which both the client and the helper perceive the problem, the helping process, and the solution. In the model we have presented, these factors are subsumed into the ethnic lens through which perceptions take place, feelings are experienced, and actions are decided upon and carried out. Similarly, we view the worker's perceptions and feelings as influenced by the lens through which both clients' and the worker's ethnic identity are viewed and experienced.

Throughout the book, we have examined the ways in which this lens can become distorted. Preconceived attitudes, prejudices, stereotypes, and past experiences can affect both the helper and the client. The result can be a lack of fit between the potential client and the worker, which may, to a large extent, be the result of the distortion itself.

The foundation for effective practice with ethnic populations, whether it is with individuals, groups, or communities, rests on the knowledge and sensitivity of practitioners with regard to the backgrounds, histories, and culture of the diverse groups they seek to serve. However, these factors alone, although critical for crossing ethnic boundaries, will in themselves not suffice without the qualities of respect and genuineness.

These qualities are conveyed through both attitudes and actions that reflect the regard with which the practitioner views the group, its traditions, its customs, and its beliefs. Involving community members on planning boards and agency committees, discussing their perceptions of needs or the saliency of community issues, and listening to their suggestions and advice are means of learning about the population, displaying respect, and establishing a basis for credibility and trust.

As emphasized throughout the book, ethnicity is not a constant determinant of actions or behaviors. There is much diversity within ethnic groups, and individuals may or may not adhere to traditions or cultures. Their unique experiences and backgrounds are important determinants of their perceptions and responses. Consequently, generalizations regarding ethnic individuals based on stereotypic assumptions may not be accurate and may impede the effectiveness of the helping process.

The social worker's lens must be sensitive enough to recognize the heterogeneity that exists within seemingly homogenous ethnic groups. As an example, the experiences of Cubans vary distinctly from those of Puerto Ricans or Mexicans, while those of the Vietnamese tend to differ in many ways from those of the Koreans, the Laotians, or the Cambodians. The tendency to classify all groups together on the basis of one characteristic such as race or language clearly disregards many factors that have had and can continue to have major impacts on group members' lives. Members of the majority must be cautious in their tendency to lump together ethnic groups, who consider themselves quite distinct from others even though they may share certain ethnoracial characteristics.

Practitioners must be aware that ethnicity is often an invisible factor in identity and may only become apparent at certain times or in relation to specific issues. This is particularly true of white ethnics, whose backgrounds and cultural ties become most visible during holidays or celebrations such as St. Patrick's Day or when homelands such as Croatia or Israel become threatened. During these periods, ethnicity can become a salient part of one's identity and behavior, only to recede again when the threat dissipates.

It is particularly important to realize that patterns perceived as cultural traits or preferences may in reality be responses to years, generations, or even centuries of discrimination or oppression. A preference for familial help over professional care is often the result of a history of professional unavailability or indifference, lack of access, and poor or demeaning treatment. The resulting lack of trust in " helpers" is thus a normal socially determined response rather than the reflection of a specific cultural preference for informal help. The perception that persons do not use services because "they look after their own" is a useful justification for professional inaction.

Unfortunately, there is frequently a tendency to attribute resistance to or underutilization of services to one of two reasons, both of which are inaccurate and offensive to ethnic group members. One is to attribute such resistance to inadequacies or deficits within the members of the community. These can range from a lack of intelligence to "cultural deficits" to "different" and dysfunctional value systems. Such stereotypes act as further barriers to the development of accessible and appropriate services.

To break a cycle of professional indifference requires making services accessible and acceptable to members of an ethnic community. Given that families and informal supports frequently play major parts in persons' lives, practitioners must be prepared to incorporate members of the client's support network into the helping process. This can only occur when the lens through which the client is perceived is sensitive to the significant individuals in the person's or group's life. The worker's lens must also see the ways in which certain community norms, values, behavior patterns, and roles are adaptive to the group's specific history and traditions. Although patterns have been appropriate in the past, they may be inappropriate in the present community setting. As an example, a strict separation between the roles of men and women can be dysfunctional in contemporary American society, and efforts to maintain this separation may impede persons and groups from full participation. The social worker's task may be to help clients develop new roles and behaviors that can assist them in strengthening their adaptive behaviors and developing their resources.

In addition, the lens of the practitioner must not be distorted by ethnic myths that assume specific attitudes and behaviors, which may no longer be present. With acculturation, persons often lose allegiance to traditional customs and behaviors or find them exceedingly difficult to enact. As illustrated in the care of the elderly, families may be extremely stressed trying to meet the support needs of older relatives. Assumptions that traditional norms of filial support prevail and that ethnic families do not require assistance prevents their needs from being met.

This book has not focused on ethnic or racial groups as victims of oppression. This is not because such a view is necessarily unjustified, but rather because it is not a useful perspective for a social work practitioner. It is often a view that generates and reinforces anger and hostility rather than a mutual engagement in problem solving. The lens that focuses primarily on members of an ethnic group as victims has a difficult time seeing innate resources and abilities. Much of the work with ethnic groups involves empowering them in society and empowerment is based upon a recognition and development of group strengths. A lens that sees only problems and weaknesses cannot act as a means for empowerment.

As with all clients, it is difficult for change to take place without motivation. In working with ethnic populations, practitioners should work so as to help clients develop this incentive for change. Professionals must also recognize that change may come about slowly and that there are frequently resistances that clients and communities need to overcome within themselves. For ethnic persons, there may be an overriding feeling that one must give up the security of old ways, the comfort of traditions, the safety of known roles and expectations, the sense of protection that can come from separateness in order to assimilate and acculturate into the mainstream.

Social workers from outside of the ethnic community are faced with the problem of establishing their credibility in order to be effective at all levels of practice. One strategy for doing this is to build relationships with ethnic media, churches, business associations, and individuals in community leadership positions. Rather than trying to be sole service providers, social workers should seek to develop interorganizational relationships with ethnic agencies. These relationships can be rewarding to both participants: the "outside" social worker learns about the community and gains credibility; the ethnic agency benefits from the resources that the social worker can offer and the ties with the larger social service system.

It has long been thought that the saliency of ethnicity declines with acculturation, years in this country, and generations. However, the recent resurgence in ethnic identification associated with group rights and demands, even at very local levels, suggests that ethnicity may remain a very vital part of identity. Moreover, being "ethnic" is increasingly being identified as a positive trait, as it connotes a sense of individuality and uniqueness displayed through symbols of "ethnic pride." These individuals may be important resources in the development of programs and services for ethnic groups because such involvements offer them the opportunity to display their allegiance and adherence to a part of their identity that is often overlooked.

Policy makers and agency administrators need to be aware constantly of the ways in which their actions can have different effects on diverse groups. Policies affecting children will more strongly affect the younger Hispanic populations. Policies affecting welfare eligibility, benefits, and reforms will have a disproportionate impact on the African-American community, and changes in services for new immigrants can have a serious effect on newly arrived Jews from the former Soviet Union. For reasons like these, policies and service systems can be institutionally biased despite procedures that appear equitable and fair. The ethnic lens must be sensitive to the varying concerns and interests of ethnic groups for the future development of just and effective social services.

Social workers also need to be cognizant of the fact that ethnic patterns and group histories can be used in either a defensive or a factitious way. Being taken in or "conned" reflects a lack of skill and understanding on the part of the social worker, rather than justifiable empathy. As an example, a person who uses his or her group's history of oppression to justify violent and assaultive behavior is not acting within an ethnic tradition but is instead being manipulative. Whatever the horrors of historical oppression and tragedy, and there are many, identifying oneself as a victim is disempowering and leaves one less, rather than more, able to deal with life in the present. The social worker who defends these actions cannot instill any incentive for change.

The roots and the future of this country are in an ethnically diverse population. As discussed early in this book, ethnic groups have alternatively been accepted or rejected, praised as contributors to the country's strength or derided as a burden, sentimentalized or oppressed. Each wave of immigrants, whether from overseas or from rural areas to the cities, has undergone comparisons with their predecessors and with those claiming to be "real Americans."

These perceptions are based not so much on the groups themselves as they are on economic and social factors that categorize the newcomers according to the needs of society and the economy at specific times. By understanding the underlying factors that influence these perceptions, social workers can make major contributions toward clarifying them and thus assuring that resulting social policies are just.

Ethnicity will continue to be a major force in this country as we enter the 21st century. Social work has within its grasp the ability to play a prominent role in designing services and policies that are sensitive to ethnic individuals, groups, and communities. The extent to which these groups benefit from the resources and institutions of the greater society will depend, to a large extent, upon the permeability of the boundaries which surround them.

One of the most difficult challenges for the social work practitioner will be to make these boundaries permeable enough so that those inside can enjoy the benefits of the greater society without forfeiting their own ethnic identity. This will enable persons to maintain their own culture and traditions while also having access to outside services and resources.

Recommendations for Practice

Based upon the previous chapters, several important recommendations for social workers working with ethnically diverse populations can be made. Whatever the field or focus of the practice, practitioners should

1. Be knowledgeable about and sensitive to diverse ethnic groups and their experiences, encouraging clients who are members of ethnic communities to be their teachers with regard to cultural traditions and mores.
2. Recognize that ethnic groups are not homogeneous but contain many subgroups who may have diverse experiences and backgrounds.
3. Consider ethnic identity and its saliency in all social work assessments.
4. Understand the impact of ethnic lenses on their own perceptions as workers, as well as on the ethnic group's as clients.
5. Be aware of the boundaries that ethnicity can present and the potential impact of these boundaries on the interactions both within and across them.
6. Be knowledgeable about the positive roles that traditional behaviors and customs can play in the lives of ethnic groups.
7. Neither underestimate or overestimate the role that ethnicity can play in people's lives.
8. Be constantly aware that ethnicity can be a major factor in the perception of needs and that needs cannot be addressed until they are recognized by the specific group.
9. Realize that the helping process frequently must incorporate many persons, including members of the immediate family, as well as community leaders who carry prestige.

Research

Research on ethnicity in social work practice is still in the beginning stages. There is an urgent need for further studies in all areas, ranging from individual case work to the effects of social policies to changes in policies. In particular, studies on innovative techniques with individuals and groups and practice outcomes are needed. Comparisons of services delivered by ethnic agencies with those by other agencies, their acceptance by individuals and communities, and the roles that they play can be crucial for further program development.

There is a great need for qualitative studies that explore the experiences of ethnic individuals and families and the meanings of these experiences in today's society. For example, the experiences of older immigrants, whose traditional roles as sources of knowledge quickly become obsolete in the acculturation process, have been little studied and are poorly understood. This type of research can provide important insight into issues and concerns faced by specific groups, which is usually not generated by other types of research.

Qualitative research can also assist in our understanding of how prospective ethnic clients perceive potential helpers and the helping process. This type of information is critical for the development of appropriate assessments and interventions.

Studies on the assimilation process of new ethnic groups can be helpful in understanding the particular dilemmas and problems that new immigrants encounter. Such studies can help in identifying the factors which facilitate integration into the society, as well as those which act as barriers. Cross-cultural studies that compare diverse ethnic groups, as well as studies of different age groups, are needed for the development of appropriate services.

Focus groups can be a particularly useful item in working with ethnic populations, as they offer a valuable means of eliciting the perceptions of group members regarding specific topics. For example, in planning mental health services for a community, groups within it can provide needed information about how mental health is viewed and how services are likely to be perceived. These groups can be important indicators of the extent of consensus within a community and the factors that can contribute to a program's success.

As ethnic groups seek greater representation in society, an active role for social workers may be in helping to develop coalitions among different groups. Such organizations could be important frameworks for political power because they serve to unite persons behind common issues. Action research into the evolution of interethnic associations that focuses on the outcomes and effectiveness of various strategies for participation and empowerment would provide sound guidance for social work involvement.

Finally, there is no conflict between a strong and meaningful ethnic identity and a full membership in the broader society. These two are, in fact, complementary. For people who are identified with an ethnic group, the one is prerequisite to the other. The complex process of acculturation vividly illustrates the fact that one cannot form a productive and contributory identity with the broader society by denying or dulling one's own heritage. Our diverse society requires that skilled social work practitioners understand the significance and impact of ethnicity on individuals and groups so that just policies and effective services can be developed. It is only through the sensitivity of the ethnic lens that the barriers frequently associated with ethnicity may be removed, so that all persons are given the opportunity to equitably participate in American society.

Index